THE
MONSTER
UNDER THE BED

Uncovering the
LIE
That Drives Us

Illustrated by Kory Muscato

BY
KIM FISKE

Advance Praise for *The Monster Under the Bed*

"Kim Fiske goes where others won't. She speaks with raw honesty and puts 'voice' to what we're thinking but won't say, even to ourselves. *The Monster Under the Bed* shines a light on the things that divide us and provides unbiased strategies for creating peace."

— Kevin W. McCarthy, author of *The On-Purpose Person* and professional speaker

"Kim's monster metaphor has taken me on a journey of self-discovery and has helped me uncover things about myself of which I was unaware. This book and Kim's teachings have literally opened up an entire new world of possibility of growth and understanding for me. It gets my highest recommendation."

— Dr. Michael Smith, Medical Director and Chief Medical Editor of WebMD

"Kim Fiske has zeroed in on and uncovered what we can DO with the voice in our head that stops us from ultimately finding the peace and fulfillment we were created for. I've been waiting for this message for over 20 years and didn't even know it!"

— Deni Robinson, Presidential Diamond Executive, Asea

"For the seeker of success, happiness, and fulfillment, *The Monster Under the Bed* provides many insights and strategies that will help you overcome your fears and limitations. Great read!"

— TJ Hoisington, author of *If You Think You Can!* and *Return to Robinson Island*

Project Management:
Creative Apogee, shannon@creativeapogee.com

Cover Design: Creative Apogee

Illustrations: Kory Muscato

Inside Layout: Ljiljana Pavkov

Printed in the United States of America

FIRST EDITION

ISBN: 978-1-7325-630-0-1 (international trade paper edition)

ISBN: 978-1-7325630-1-8 (eBook)

Published by Metamind Press

Table of Contents

THE
MONSTER
UNDER THE BED

There is really only one person to whom I would dedicate this book: My husband, Joe Fiske. He has truly been the most supportive, patient, and emphatic about my finishing this book.

He has witnessed my monster first hand - and has also grown with me as I have talked his ear off with all of my discoveries and ideas.

He is the wind beneath my wings, for sure!

I love you!

Kim

Special Thanks!

I'd also like to acknowledge these people for all the help, support, proofing, and suggestions during the writing of this book:

Kathi Myers - my sister, my right arm and best friend!

Kris Wente - my 2nd born and a major contributor to this book

Keith Reed - my brother and someone who would listen, learn, grow and love simultaneously

Sally Cheney - A dear friend who spent a good chunk of time helping me clarify these principles

Christine Whitemarsh - A book coach and friend

Jere McGrew, Jenny Berg, Jamil Frasier, Dr. Kelly Rife - for their sacrifice of time to help me tweak thoughts and principles.

To *Kris, Catherine, Nathan* and *Lindsey Wente,* and *Steven* and *Prosper Fiske* - For the love and openness that is in our family culture.

Braydan, Tes, Vann, Kash and *Eve Wente.* You guys gave me the extra "propellant" to write this book. I want you to have a roadmap to see your monster, when you're ready, and to know how to navigate life with it always by your side.

When it takes over 2 years to write a book, the chance of leaving someone out who provided valuable and treasured input is probable. Please know that I love and appreciate your contribution.

Kim Fiske

Foreword

I admit I did a double take. The FedEx guy was...a lady... perhaps the first delivery woman I had ever seen; it was 1988 – don't judge! So, I wondered who she was that she would apply, get hired, and actually love being the FedEx lady. Every time she brought a delivery, I found myself peering into her mind and heart, curious to understand what made her tick.

She seemed to love the work. Or maybe she just loved her customers. Or maybe she just loved. She was always so on fire – even if it was about the envelope she had so passionately curated for me.

As I got to know her better through just being curious enough to ask, I learned about her husband, Joe, and the boys. And I learned quickly that what burned inside this lady boss could never be harnessed by FedEx or any other restrictive corporate culture. She had vision.

She was going somewhere big. She didn't really know where, but that did not dampen her conviction.

Kim Fiske was destined to be an entrepreneur, a leader of leaders, a teacher, and a coach. Writing a book about the journey and the wisdom gained is just an afterthought, kind of like a cool Facebook post after an epic day.

I offered her the opportunity to go beyond the truck in the early 1990s. She took to it like a runner in the blocks, gun fired. She sprinted to stardom, producing record-setting results and being a passionate servant-leader for her sales team.

My opportunity was not even big enough for her, and before long she leapt out into the big world to find her own way. I watched Kim from afar for about a decade. She took on some huge opportunities, succeeding, failing, and falling forward every time. The FedEx truck was light years in her rear-view mirror. She always had big vision and was always looking to find "home", one that would fill that huge space she held in her heart for leadership and service.

And then, like everyone that stays true to their vision and fights for its fruition, Kim Fiske hit pay dirt. She recruited, trained, and motivated a team of hundreds of coaches in a highly competitive business – weight loss. I cannot think of a harder psychological challenge than motivating and coaching people to achieve and sustain significant weight loss. It must be like herding cats. Kim's competitive edge is her passion for coaching people like herself – people with the spark of being someone greater – to learn to believe in that upside and go for it.

Kim has coached hundreds of entrepreneurs and thousands of customers to pure transformation. Her business has earned her over $1M a year for several years now and, true to form, Kim created this empire with great balance and freedom. She has never had an office or employees. Mostly she enjoys her family, new business interests, travel, fitness, and continued learning. She is the essence of a role model.

This book contains the distinctions, skills, beliefs, and wisdom that have ultimately become Kim Fiske's secret weapon. She learned them. You can too. And if I condensed this powerhouse-of-a-leader down to one quality, she wants you to learn these secrets too.

Richard Bliss Brooke

Preface

The overall message of this book has been in my life for quite a while. I've learned that there are scary things in the world that live only in my head. This is what I have coined as *the monster*. I've sensed that these scary things have impacted and affected every area of my life, for as long as I can remember. I know there are thoughts that say negative things to us that we believe, unless we are given tools to combat them.

These voices have reached into every part of each of our lives. I've seen the havoc they wreak in our relationships, our physical bodies, our mental health and our emotional well-being. I'm also convinced all of these areas are connected. When one area is awry, the others follow suite.

As you will read in my history, music and performing were pillars since childhood. I've a performed and directed music and theater for most of my life. Part of my leadership development over the years was my ability to inspire and manage large groups of people in choirs and theater productions I directed. It was in these roles that I saw my monster first-hand and as a result lost some important relationships along the way

I've also been in the relationship marketing profession for the better part of 35 years. I have recruited, trained, and coached hundreds of people during these years; the most recent experience being with a health and weight loss company. I have helped train and mentor several people whose businesses earn multiple six-figure incomes.

Despite these successes, I have seen the "good, bad and the ugly" in regard to the monster I'm addressing in this book. It is the voice we hear that dresses itself up as truth. It's a trickster, and we have bought into this voice hook, line and sinker. The illusive feeling of satisfaction that is expected to be waiting for us at the end of the proverbial rainbow rarely, if ever, came.

The final "straw" for me is the political situation we find ourselves in. I am seeing the damage people's *monsters* are creating; the families who are being ripped apart, and close friends who no longer speak to each other. This eats at my soul. Even though the idea of this book has been brewing in the background for a couple of years, the current situation has thrown the necessary *fuel on the fire* to get this message out as soon as I can.

My ultimate desire for this book is for people to have peace in their hearts, lives, and relationships. Although

I've read many books, articles, and studies regarding brain development, I'm not citing many sources for this work – which is based on everything I've understood from academia as well as the personal and professional experiences in my life and business coaching. The ideas, principles, and tools I put forward here are forged first-hand, starting with myself, and subsequently, in the trenches with real people, in real-life situations.

My suggestion is to try this information on for yourself. How does it feel? Does it resonate with you? I am not proposing this is the *truth*. You are free to agree or disagree. You could hold it as an allegory or even a fairy tale. This may help you hear the message more easily.

I've intentionally left room for greater understanding to follow as I deepen my awareness. I personally believe that true learning never stops. If you are reading this and there is a pull to find peace in your life and relationships – and you are willing to look "under the bed" AND in the mirror for a new understanding of your life – this book can be the starting point.

Introduction

As a child I suffered many sleepless nights disturbed by the monster under my bed. I was afraid of this monster; in fact, I was terrified. The monster was real. It was there. It was going to get me. That was my truth.

I was never sure of the monster's intent, but the reason a monster would live under a child's bed while she slept alone in the dark could not be good! It became impossible for me to relax. My mind would race with scenarios. How would I fight the monster off should it attack? How could my covers protect me from a living, breathing, and hungry monster under my bed?

What was worse, was there was no escape. I would lie there paralyzed by fear that I would squirm, and the monster would know I was there. So, I would sweat, feeling my heart pound through my chest, along with the dread of having to get up to relieve a full bladder.

I remember clearly trying to talk myself out of having to pee, and maybe sometimes I did; but I have a clearer memory of trying to figure out how to run to the bathroom so as to not get caught by the monster.

I also pictured over and over again what would happen if I fell asleep and unknowingly exposed any part of me to that scary creature below. Night after night, I was careful to keep each of my limbs securely on the mattress and safe beneath the covers. I knew that if I let an arm or a leg escape from the boundaries of the bed, even accidentally, they'd be gobbled up. Wide-eyed and silent, my heartbeat pulsing in my eardrums, I would listen for any signs that confirmed my worst suspicions.

I could not call for help. Nobody would believe me. They would just tell me monsters weren't real; but they didn't know, and they weren't the ones left alone at the monster's mercy. In the morning, the monster would surely be gone; but everyone knows monsters hide at first sign of light. Throughout the day, I was dreading

the moment just after being tucked in, when my mom would turn out my light, when I would be, once again, defenseless, vulnerable, and afraid.

The monster never got me; but that just meant I lived to die another day. There would be another, and another, and another. That was until one day, with my developing cognitive mind and a wildly beating heart, I lifted the bedspread and found nothing beneath the bed other than a few harmless dust bunnies and some dirty socks. I knew then that the monster was not real. Nothing was there that would get me; however, those sleepless nights were real. The fear was also real, as was the dread, and so were the long hours of agony in the dark because of the monster I created.

Little did I know, this was not the end of my monster...

Even as adults, we sense something "underneath our bed," hiding from any light so as not to be seen; but just like our childhood monster, we don't want to face it, for fear of death. We're not always sure why we feel the way we do; why we feel conflicted between our logical brain and our emotions; why we see dysfunctional patterns play themselves out over and over; and why we have continual conflict in our most important relationships. All we know is how helpless and powerless we are. We only feel the fear, dread and anxiety.

I've discovered that no matter how successful, put-together, or wealthy someone seems, everyone has a feeling inside them, a fear of something hiding under their proverbial bed. It's the feeling: *I'm not acceptable; I'm not worthy; I'm not deserving; I'm not loveable - just as*

I am. What the monster whispers is: *I'm not okay at the deepest part of my being.* Our lives unfold with the results of this belief. And we metaphorically hold in our breath, tuck under the blankets tighter, and hope, hope, hope we don't have to pee.

This book is for those who:

- Have a sense that there is something under the "covers" of their psyche but don't know what it is or how to access it.
- Are willing to look at their thoughts instead of believing them.
- Are tired of the pain in their life and relationships.
- Are ready to do the internal work to find peace.

My goals with this book are to help:

- Bring awareness to areas of conflict in our lives.
- Determine whether there is a monster under our bed.
- Understand how our monster was created.
- Understand the monster's purpose - both then and now.
- Discover what can be done about it.

The following chapters will deepen this metaphor. Our monster arose precisely from our younger brain, though, unlike our belief in Santa or the Easter Bunny, the monster stuck. While other childhood myths were explained away, most of us have not had the proper tools to question the decisions and beliefs deeply embedded in our early years. The adults in our lives during these early years had no idea about how the young brain developed. And because they were still dealing with the monster in their own psyche, they were ill-equipped to deal with ours as we grew.

Our adult lives are frequently in constant inner conflicts that result in anxiety, depression, anger, unforgiveness, and self-loathing. The world in which we live has abnormally high stress, family issues, job and financial insecurities, technological acceleration, and it continually tests our personal and spiritual boundaries – all of this exacerbating the already heightened fear, which in turn triggers our monster. The spiral continues on and on.

We still believe in monsters. They have different forms and speak, at times, through our deepest and most trusted voices. They have told us things that we *know* to be **true**, so we lay awake, unable to move, fearful one misstep could end in a gruesome reality. But come with me. We will go together, lift up the bedspread, and run headlong to the monster's roar. Like me, you may start to realize that the scary monster was only your dust bunnies and dirty socks, too.

Chapter 1

The Birth of the Monster

We are born with amazing abilities that are primarily concerned with our survival. Our main survival tactic was crying when we needed food, water, comfort, and rest. But cognitively we are not given any tools that involve reason and logic – at least not yet. As we start to grow, we develop through a process of imitating. We learn to first make sounds, move our bodies, discover eye contact, notice smiles, and, unknowingly, we are making emotional connections. This requires no effort on our part. It is as natural as our basic physical capabilities of development – such as growing hair and nails, digesting food, and breathing.

We don't understand *logically* what our parents are saying to us, during our baby years, but we can sense *emotionally* when they are happy or unhappy with our actions, which is where our mental and emotional programming starts.

In these early years, we are primarily guided by our amygdala – which lives in our survival brain. From an evolutionary standpoint, it is the oldest part of our brain – which is emotional, nonverbal, and reactive. It is on high alert and ever watchful. It wants to keep us fed, safe, and warm. It doesn't deal with logic.

The prefrontal cortex, the logical or reasoning brain, doesn't fully develop until the mid-twenties. Did you ever wonder why car insurance rates reduce once the driver is 25 year old, and why most car rental agencies require the renter to be at least, 25 years old? They understand this development.

There is another little known or talked about survival need we are born with. We are born with an instinctual need to belong; to be accepted in our social community. It's in our DNA. We are a social species and we need our community as much, if not more, than food and water. We don't logically know we have this need yet well, because we don't logically know anything yet. This need lives in the non-verbal place. In fact, this is the main issue I will be dealing with in this book.

In the 1950s, at the University of Oregon, Harry Harlow examined the need for love and belonging through observing rhesus monkeys. Constructing two types of "mothers" – one made of wire mesh and a bottle, the other covered in terry cloth and more closely resembling the monkey's real mother – Harlow observed how the monkeys reacted to each. He observed that the monkeys preferred to spend time cuddling and nuzzling the terry cloth "mother", even when their nourishment came from the other source.

When he introduced a fear element in the form of a teddy bear banging a drum, the monkeys with the terry-cloth surrogate clung to the cloth, touched it, and could resume play after the threat had gone. The monkeys without the warm and nurturing mother, took longer to calm down and would huddle by themselves for long periods of time. Without the assurance of being loved and cared for, fear became more threatening and more difficult to overcome. Harlow concluded that **the desire for nurture was even stronger than the need for nourishment.** Attachment was more important than satisfying hunger and thirst.

Somewhere in our young, illogical brain, we made deep emotional decisions about who we were, which affects our identity for the rest of our lives.

Exclusion could mean death. We could not have evolved in solitude. We must have our community. Our amygdala knows this and is fully functioning at birth to make sure we survive – and acceptance is a key component of our survival.

Somewhere in our young, illogical brain, we made deep emotional decisions about who we were, which affects our identity for the rest of our lives. When a thought is accompanied by strong emotions, our brain holds it as the **truth**. The fear that we aren't somehow acceptable turns out to be the foundation of our entire life. Everyone who is a part of our social community, and everything we experience as we grow, is processed and judged emotionally, albeit illogically, according to this question: **Am I acceptable?** *(Aka - Will I be able to survive?)*

Oprah Winfrey confirmed this in an interview she gave at Stanford's business school. When the young woman interviewing her asked who the most interesting person was that she had ever interviewed, Oprah said, "I don't know about that, but the universal question everybody asked when done being interviewed was, Was that okay? And guess what I will ask you when we are done with this interview – Was that okay?" Yes, even Oprah asks that question.

At some point the thought that we are **not okay** created intense fear. Our amygdala processes fear as a precursor to death. So, this thought led to the feeling **I could die**. This strong emotion of fear imprinted on our psyche and started the mental wiring we are products of today. This is what I will refer to in this book as our **lie**. The lie tells us that we don't deserve the love we have and want, that we aren't sufficient the way we are.

It is this lie that births the monster. In fact, I will use these words synonymously. Sure, maybe no one else can see it; but we are convinced that it is there. It is fear embodied. It is the lie made flesh. And **it is terrifying**.

It's All about Us!

We are conditioned to see the world through the lens of how things affect us. We can't help this. Our early brain circuitry is wired with the notion that everything that happens **to us** is *because of us*. If we didn't have this perception, in the big scheme of evolution, we could die. Our natural survival programming has us on high alert for how all things will impact *us* in our quest for survival.

We aren't wired to think of others during this phase of life. That would take a developed prefrontal cortex brain. It is even hard for us now, with our adult brain, to go back *to* those early years to understand our child brain. It makes no sense, so therefore what I'm proposing here may seem ridiculous with the brain you are using to read and understand with.

The amygdala's primary job is to keep us on high alert and conscious of how everything that happens around us is related to us. We are left ill-equipped to process information accurately about ourselves at these critical ages. When our younger selves felt the threat of not being acceptable in our community, it sparked a deep fear. When that happened, our biggest survival ally, our amygdala, (heretofore referred to as *Amy*), was summoned.

If you could go back with me to imagine when, for example, you were suddenly yanked away from a hot stove, or from running out into the street, or scolded for attempting to pet a stray dog. What mental equipment did you have to process that? Without your logical, reasoning brain, you had no clue that your mother or father loved you so much and they knew you were in danger, so they reacted with fear to keep you safe. Instead, all you felt was their reaction, which to your child brain meant something was wrong - with **YOU**.

These people are yelling at me, even hitting me. I don't know what I did, but I could die, was the **feeling** that was produced.

Remember, the non-verbal, non-stop, question running in the background was, *"Am I acceptable? Am I loved? Will I be included in this tribe?"* The emotional Amy's answer was a resounding **"NO! Danger Danger Will Robinson!"**

It would take the part of your brain you didn't have access to, to process it any differently. This is why many times children of divorce or sexual abuse have it wired that what happened to them was **their fault**. They had no way to logically think it through. They didn't have that brain developed yet and when that brain was fully developed, the faulty circuitry had already been laid. *They were already aligned with the **lie**.*

When I was four years old, my mom and dad got divorced. My adult brain knows that my dad didn't want to be married to my mom anymore. But little Kimmy had it wired that he left **HER!** She wasn't good enough and if she had been different somehow, this wouldn't have happened. I also processed the pain my mom was in during this time as something of my doing. *Somehow, if I was **better**, my mom wouldn't be crying so much.*

Children have no other choice but to see everything as connected to and, potentially, caused by themselves.

Even as adults, we can see this thought process play out. When someone says or does something, we automatically process it with **how does this apply to me?** Now that I'm aware of this tendency in myself, I hear it constantly throughout conversations in which I take part. I watch for this wiring running in my background, and I can override it. Children have no other choice but to see everything as connected to and, potentially, caused by themselves.

Triggering the Monster

Amy, sensing fear and potential death, sends the message to our brain: *DO SOMETHING! Quick!* We know this as *flight or fight*. We have an *automatic* reaction to this lie; to this monster. And the only way to survive this is for our brains, illogical or not, to get busy with survival mechanisms that will ensure we are okay and accepted – and therefore, **we won't die.** Amy is automatically geared with the *flight or fight* responses that we need. Even though it seems the lie is in the core of everyone I've ever met or worked with, how that lie plays out doesn't follow any logical pattern.

Amy doesn't reason with us. It doesn't ask our young self if what we're thinking, or feeling is true. It doesn't try to convince us that we are unconditionally loved and accepted by our parents, or help explain the monsters they are dealing with. It doesn't explain that maybe the yelling, anger and fear our parent felt towards us was a sign that they loved us. It doesn't show us the monsters our siblings are fighting, which could explain their behavior toward us.

With regard to siblings, they can contribute a large role in the conception that we are **not okay** and the embedding of our lie. Two siblings raised in the same home by the same parents will process things completely differently; but it is important to remember that our siblings are dealing with their newly created monster too! They don't quite know what to do with this new little ball of joy and love that just entered and wreaked havoc on their worlds – otherwise known as **you.**

A brief example of how siblings impact one's monster is my friend Ryan and his brother two years older, Bobby. Their parents have always been into sports, and excelling in athletics was a clear virtue in their household. Bobby was gifted in sports and enjoyed playing in different leagues year-round, often as a starter or captain. Ryan knew Bobby was good, even without everyone praising him continually. Ryan, wanting his parents to accept him too, worked hard to prove his worth in sports, but his skill never matched that of his champion older brother.

At this juncture, Ryan was faced with a choice. He could use this fact to beat himself up, as some do, and never excel at anything. Or he could say *forget it* to sports and find his own niche in which to excel. He would never beat Bobby at his own game, or games. But he could find another avenue where he could shine his own light – and not be in Bobby's shadow.

Ryan had something to prove. Or believed he did. There is so much proving happening in these things. We are either proving the lie as true - *that I suck* - or proving it **untrue** by having to win at all costs, thereby still proving the lie as functional **truth**.

Once you are aware of these patterns, it's interesting to watch them play out. Awareness is one of the goals of this book. Once aware, you can access the tools to make new decisions and rewire new brain pathways that align with who you want to be and who you really are.

Any and all trauma triggers our survivalist, Amy. And it reacts, born from our fear, fully-armored and ready to protect us against any threat, real or perceived. Amy only feels what we feel and responds with survival messages, when the feeling is intense. *To Amy, intense fearful emotions can only mean one thing: Death is imminent!*

In this metaphor, the imagined monster came from the lie that we might not be good enough and could be outcast from our community. This fear sparks Amy's very real survival instincts. *Amy doesn't have logic or understanding of the truth. Our feeling is Amy's truth.* The only message it hears is the *feeling* of fear, anxiety, stress, apprehension, panic, and the like. The only message it can respond with is *flight* or *fight*. When we feel fear, it assumes it's real and gets busy saving us.

And how does one deal with an invisible and illogical foe? Amy doesn't know exactly, but it can get creative. It only knows to come up with survival mechanisms to help us be accepted and loved, to fit into our social environment, per our survival requirements.

We can see Amy's role clearly in these *flight or fight* messages. The *flight* message might be to *retreat* because we aren't good/smart/worthy enough. This *flight* message perpetuates the negative emotions and therefore triggers Amy anew and this time we receive a *fight* message - *Oh yeah?!...I'll show you!* as we go on being driven by the monster to win, succeed, earn, prove, etc. But when we try to prove a lie wrong, we end up just confirming that we really believe it's true. We keep seeking the approval we never needed.

The truth is: **We can never get enough of what we never needed to begin with.**

In other words, we will *always* crave that which we never needed. We will ever be seeking, but never finding. It's faulty wiring. The message that I needed to **DO** something to be loved and accepted was never true. Until we do the necessary emotional rewiring using our high powered prefrontal cortex brain to investigate this unconscious belief, we will continually feel less than, inadequate and lacking.

When we feel the lie brewing inside us, the monster is triggered. It scares us with the same feeling we had when we were young and illogical. It doesn't know that we are now an adult with a reasoning brain. Our young child self is holding us hostage emotionally.

Regardless of pinpointing the exact time or specific experience that this lie was embedded within us (even if we could), it still informs our thoughts, actions, and fears more than we know. These emotions started the circuitry in our brain. It started creating the operating system that would dictate, decide and drive the rest of our lives. The stronger the emotion behind the experience, the stronger the firing in our brain. Emotions are part of the wiring circuitry of our brains – *what fires together, wires together* – and we've been illogically wired since childhood without even knowing it.

Do you know any four-year-old to whom you would trust your life? Yet, the truth is we have all done precisely that. Without our realizing it, our emotional and neurological pathways have been created and embedded by our half-brained self. The good news is that the lie is as real as the monsters under the bed of our childhood imagination – totally fabricated. We just don't know it, until now.

The Ego

If you pick up most personal development books or attend any enlightenment seminars, the subject of the ego will usually be addressed. Our egos reflect our personal identity, and when our identity is shaky, we will dig in and puff up.

When we think of someone with a big ego, or an egotist, what we have experienced is their monster in full attack mode. It's the need to ensure people know how good/perfect/worthy they are. The genesis stemming, again, from the monster.

Ego is defined as *the view that a person has of themselves.* Period. The majority of people, if asked to give a definition of ego, wouldn't give this Freudian textbook definition. They would say it is something to be eliminated or to be overcome. Growing up in church, the ego was equated with the "flesh," the "old man," pride. It has always had a negative connotation. There is even a definition using it as an acronym: Edging God Out.

Where did the interpretation come from that ego means something bad? Who decided this? And why do so many people in the world seem to agree with this definition? It's as if this word has the meaning we, as a collective, give it. We decided, based on our experiences with our own egos (our self-concept) that it is bad.

The fact that everyone's concept of self is a negative one, and it's viewed as something to be tamed, changed, or even eliminated, shows me the true picture people have of themselves. And if anyone threatens our ego, real or perceived, we will move heaven and earth to protect it. I'll be addressing more about this later in the book.

Monster Strategies

Amy gets our survival strategies from our environment. If our family values sports (like Ryan and

Bobby's family), our survival tactics will develop into being athletic and fast, winning at all costs, beating the competition. If our family values intelligence, we learn quickly that we must get straight As or at least go to college. If we have perfectionist parents, perfection will be the path for us. If our family heritage is in the armed forces or in public service, we will be drawn to the military, police, or firefighters. If our family is musical, we'll be taking piano lessons, guitar lessons, etc. to prove our worth in our community. Get the picture? It's no wonder I was singing and performing at such a young age. That's what was valued in my family. Amy was guiding me perfectly.

Linda, a client and close friend of mine, has an interesting story that shows how something untrue can still shape one's world, one's actions, and one's very sense of self. You see, Linda had a traumatic childhood. She was told all throughout her life that she'd been abused by her father – who was a "Satan worshiper" and who "ran a sex trafficking ring."

She lived in hiding through her young life with her mom and brother – always on the run. This story was reinforced in many ways. For example, Linda once had a pain in her eye, and she was told it was because her eye was stuck with a pin during her abuse. Any physical discomfort throughout her entire life was immediately followed with her mind making the familiar connection and telling her that it was because she was abused.

It wasn't until many years later – when Linda was an adult – that she began to question some of the things she'd grown up "knowing." Her logical brain now developed, she began the search to reconnect with her father. Even though a huge part of her was still extremely scared, something deeper told her to keep looking.

When she wrote to her father, she hid all information about her whereabouts and her new married name – or that she now had a child of her own. There was still too much risk to trust this man yet. But she found him, which, inversely, meant that he had now found her. And she learned that he had been looking for her and her brother all of their lives.

He wasn't searching so he could kill them; he was trying to find them because he loved them. He had missed them, had longed for them, and had borne their absence like an open wound for the better part of three decades. After the truth emerged, Linda had to reconcile what she had believed for so long with what she had now discovered.

Her entire identity in every area of her life was built on a lie.

A counselor told Linda that it really didn't matter that she was never physically abused; the damage done to her deep psyche made it as if she had been. As the realization unfolded in her mind – what was real versus what she grew up believing – she recalled moments when decisions she made in her life stemmed from the elaborate and traumatic falsehoods she had been told. Basically, her entire identity in every area of her life was built on a lie.

Her monster, therefore, produced many productive behaviors – as is the case for all of us. But as the light of what actually happened began to break through, she found herself building an entirely new context for her life. She was not a **victim.** She had *not* been violated. So, she did not need to guard herself so tightly. She could *trust* people.

This is a great example of how the lie works inside of us. When we **align** with, or, believe the lie, the monster creates survival mechanisms to help us live. It doesn't really know or care what the actual truth is. It becomes *our truth* as we follow these *emotionally-laid* neural pathways. Luckily, Linda used her logical brain when she was an adult to examine and question the things she had believed were true. She, eventually, was able to overcome years of misbelief. Today, Linda and her dad are connected and have a great relationship.

Again, it doesn't matter what actually happened or when the lie was embedded. It could make **zero** logical sense and not be true at all, or it could have been created from real-life abuse or even perceived abuse, as the story of Linda details. However the internal lie was produced, the strategies put forth in this book and the work we do, provide a mental framework to heal our internal wounds, be they illogical or real – they are real to us no matter what.

Note to Parents:

First of all, take comfort. Can you see that even if we raised our children perfectly (whatever *that* means), their ability to process things accurately, from a logical perspective, was impaired? For those of you who may be beating yourselves up, fearing you've ruined your kids, take comfort in knowing *no one escapes childhood without the effects of their illogical fears.* We (and therefore our children) are inevitably doomed (and blessed) to have the monster's influence in the deepest part of our psyche.

Does that mean it doesn't matter what parents do? It absolutely does. If you still have children at home, being aware of how monsters are created and being mindful of your actions and words can make a huge difference. A part of me would love the chance to go back with what I know now and have a do-over; but the best thing we can do for our children *now* is to identify and heal *our* wounds, defang our monsters, love ourselves, and set the example for what our children will want to do in their own lives – when they are ready.

My Lie

I was the youngest of three children. My mom and dad were ministers in a large protestant denomination and had a traveling music ministry prior to my being born.

They divorced when I was four. My mom kept us in church and we grew up singing, playing instruments, and performing. My sister, Kathi, and my brother, Keith, and I were close growing up and all extremely strong-willed.

The environment in our home in the '60s and '70s, after the divorce, was very hurtful between the sparring sides of my family. My maternal grandparents were constantly negative regarding my dad, and some of my dad's family had nothing good to say about my mom. Since we lived primarily with our mom, we grew up closer to her side of the family.

I was at the ripe age for monster development during the rough years preceding and following the divorce. I don't have a conscious memory of when I embedded my lie, but I was already deep into my twenties when I began noticing the tracks of the monster in my life. I had an insatiable need to be *special*. The thought of being average – or like everyone else – was unthinkable!

I probably decided that if I had been more *special*, my dad wouldn't have left me. As an adult, of course, I know now that my dad left my mom. But Little-Kimmy didn't feel that way. Why would she? Everything was about her and because of her! My dad had left me for another woman, and therefore I had it wired that I wasn't *special* enough.

Initially, the flight message reflects the original lie or a variation of it. It is telling me why **I'm not good enough**; for me, that was my not being *special* enough:

- I'm not as *pretty* as my sister, Kathi.

- I can't *play the piano* like my friend, Kathy Paul
- I can't *sing* like my friend, Kathy Paul
- I can't *play and sing together* like my friend, Kathy Paul
- I can't *perform* like my friend, Kathy Paul
- I am not as *funny* as my sister, Kathi

(Interesting how these "Kathi/Kathy's" influenced my life!)

So, my Amy got to work. It drove me with *fight* messages to prove how *special* I was. It told me, **Kim, you better:**

- Play the piano
- Sing
- Sing while playing the piano!
- Perform
- Be funny
- Draw a ton of attention to yourself
- Make sure people think you're *special*
- Be pretty so boys will like you!

I vacillated between the *flight* and *fight* messages regularly.

Notice how I didn't compare myself to my brother, Keith – who was also very talented. He was a boy, and that kind of special didn't matter; it was the female variety of special that mattered. Remember, my dad left me for another woman! That was at the heart of my monster!

I am five years younger than my sister, Kathi. She was always the beautiful and funny one. She had amazing skin. She could tan. She had perfect teeth, after my mom found a way to afford her to have braces. She had big, dreamy eyes. People would stare at her and comment how beautiful Kathi was wherever we went. She had a way with hair, makeup, clothes, and decorating; these were not my strengths. I had bad teeth, plain hair, no fashion sense, and freckles. My jokes fell flat. I noticed early on that I definitely was not as *special* as Kathi.

I remember when I was a teenager acknowledging that I was never going to be more *special* than Kathi in many ways; but maybe I could make up for it in other ways. I don't remember now what those things were specifically; but I believe that mindset is what drew me into the personal development and the leadership world.

Let me clarify again about the *special* distinction I'm referring to. I'm not talking about how everyone is unique and **special** in their own intrinsic way. I'm not talking about how I may have talents that people find appealing. The *special* I'm talking about is **monster driven**. It's a *fight* strategy stemmed from the *flight* message that came from the illogical fear that I'm not good enough. My variation of *not good enough* was that I was *average*, nothing *special*.

My teenage years were spent with my hormones and my monster in full-blown control. I was completely boy crazy. I dabbled in sports and played a little volleyball, but mainly to wear the booty shorts (I did have good legs!) to get any attention I could. I wore make up early, which was **not** the custom for a "good Christian girl" in the late '60s. I developed early. I was tall and mature for my age. This all played out nicely in my *attention-getting* *ploy.* I was headstrong, but a dumb blonde when it suited my "boy purposes." **It was just never enough.**

I had my first real love in my junior and senior year in high school. Alas, he was older and was off to college, and he left me behind fairly quickly. He was just another man leaving me because I wasn't *special* enough!

To prove my *specialness* after that, I decided to get married! That would prove it! A good-looking guy took interest in me and – even though it was based completely on the monster and my hurt heart – we were married when I was 18 years old, fresh out of high school. We had Nathan a year later. We had Kristopher five years after that. This was about the time my prefrontal brain was finishing developing and I basically "changed my mind" about what I wanted.

I was still not *special* enough and was unhappy in that marriage. (Of course, I was. I was unhappy, period.) So, I left a very nice man who probably would have never hurt me. My monster was still not satisfied. I still craved proving how *special* I was. Can you sense the inner conflict with the monster driving my life?

Shortly after I left my first husband, I met Joe – my current husband now of 31 years – in a bar! Yep! A "meat-market" type bar. I had always been a good Christian, church girl. I was feeling the need to sow some wild oats. My kids were with their dad on weekends, so that gave me time. I was Looking for Love in All the Wrong Places! I still craved my dad's love.

Joe and I were married a year later, and it was around this time when I started seeing patterns show up in my life and behavior. That recognition was the beginning of tracking the monster. (I hadn't created this metaphor or distinction yet, though.) I was in my late twenties when I identified this pull to be *special*.

I was introduced to relationship marketing and started on an intensive personal development track. I started waking up to who I was and what was holding me back. I was discovering what was possible for me. This is where I met my first mentor, Richard Brooke. It was in this arena that I started becoming aware that something was "under my bed" and seeing the driving force (the monster) of my life up to that point.

In the following chapters, I will delve deeper into this concept and show you, as well, how you can pull up your bedspread and see what's really going on. This will help you understand how we are wired – my theory of it, anyway.

> **I started waking up to who I was and what was holding me back. I was discovering what was possible for me.**

Chapter 2

Faces of
the Monster

As you lift the covers to expose the monster and expose the lie, the inherent fear will start to brew. You will usually hear the *flight* message first. The monster will have you feel *less than*, embarrassed, fearful, resonating with the shameful aspects of the lie. You will shrink back. You will even *find ways* to be unworthy, not smart, not good, all to prove in a multitude of ways that the lie is the truth. You'll engage in self-sabotage and scratch your head wondering why you continue to do what you do. It won't make any logical sense.

Some people shift to the *fight* response immediately after feeling the *flight*. They will feel they **must** prove the lie wrong. They will need to be better behaved, more productive, *worthier*, more important, smarter, prettier, etc. However, in trying to **prove** the lie wrong, they are simultaneously validating their belief in the lie.

I began *hunting my monster*. Over the years I noticed how the monster could be triggered or soothed. I noticed how sometimes I would shrink back and feel shame, and then how other times I was a bull in a china shop proving how *special* I was.

The Third F

There is the third monster response that is rarely mentioned but equally important to be aware of: to **freeze**. When you're in this freeze state, you aren't driven to prove the monster right or wrong – **you do nothing** at all. You stop. You play dead. You will recognize this if you have ever felt completely overwhelmed.

Joe and I have a morning ritual. We have our coffee in the hot tub. Our vacation home in Southern Oregon is up on a hill overlooking a beautiful view. It's like the set of *Snow White* – the deer, wild turkeys, birds, squirrels playing together right around our hot tub. Many times, we will see the "freeze" instinct in deer. You might know the expression "a deer in headlights" as describing a state of freezing from shock or apprehension – which is exactly what they do. They feel the fear and they freeze. We see it happen if we make a sudden movement getting in or out of the tub. They just stand there holding completely still.

We laugh and put words in their mouth like "If I hold still, they won't see me, right?"

This is such a common response to fear – paralysis. We haven't yet decided to *flight or fight*. So, we think. And guess where fear lives? **In our thoughts.** So, sometimes the more we think, it just ends up keeping us in the fear loop.

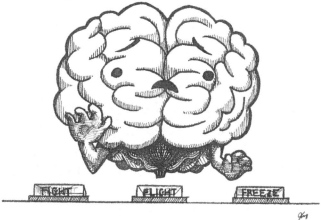

Here are some specific examples of the three F's.

Flight

- Not wanting to engage in a conversation with "smart" people.
- Needing to have everything planned out first.
- Dreading speaking in front of groups.
- Shrinking back from social gatherings.
- Worrying about what people think.
- Hesitating to try anything new.
- Avoiding confrontation and growing resentful.
- Avoiding mirrors at all costs.

Fight

- Having to ALWAYS WIN!
- Needing to be RIGHT
- Being driven to get straight A's in school.
- Seeking after perfect performance reviews.
- Becoming a top money earner.
- Needing to have a perfect body, hair, makeup, (fill in the vanity blank).
- Becoming a workaholic.
- Exhibiting obsessive behavior.

Freeze

- Spending endless time scrolling social media.
- Watching TV or movies in a daze.
- Playing Candy Crush by the hour.
- Doing meaningless things to avoid thinking about what really needs to be done.
- Procrastinating.

If you find yourself engaging in any of the above responses, pause a moment (I didn't say freeze), and examine them. Most of the time these arise as a **reaction** rather than an intent. And you wouldn't engage Amy in helping you survive unless there was a trigger present – usually, one you attempt to avoid.

The *flight*, *fight*, and *freeze* responses are important to notice. They lead us to greater understanding. Pay attention to the energy you feel - any time you feel stuck, resistant or extremely driven. That could be your friendly neighborhood Amy protecting you from something - and that *something* could be connected to the lie.

Ron's Story

One particular CEO I worked with, Ron, told me a story of how his mother left his dad, rather suddenly, when Ron was very young. This resulted in Ron's father being devastated. He cried often. He was angry toward Ron's mom and didn't hide his grief or anger from Ron. This resulted in a traumatic event for Ron. He felt conflicted on both counts. His mom, whom he loved, couldn't be bad, and his dad, whom he loved, hurt. As all kids do, Ron **knew** both of these things were *because of him*. He concluded that **he was *bad*.**

He heard this lie whispering from *under his bed*. So, Ron compensated to disprove the lie. Ron determined he would get good grades in school, be a virgin until marriage, be a leader in his church, be successful in his career, and so forth.

But these behaviors did not work. Ron still felt he was *bad* inside. And while Ron was fighting to "be good," he had a huge amount of self-judgment toward any behavior that he deemed as *bad*. He was in a no-win situation for internal peace.

Sarah's Story

Another client I worked with, Sarah, discovered her lie was that she was *dumb*, so her survival mechanism was to be *smart*. When she was about five years old, her favorite book was *Are You My Mother?* by Dr. Seuss. She loved it so much that she memorized every single line. She even told anyone who would listen that she could read, and then she would recite the book from memory.

She even showed off to her grandma when she visited and pretended she was reading the book; but she just had memorized all the words so her grandma would think she was smart. The common fear that accompanies a *flight* strategy is that we will be found out to be the phony we are. This was part of Sarah's conditioning as well.

When Sarah was in the second grade, one day her teacher announced that she would read *Are You My Mother?* aloud to the class. Sarah sat there, head held high and **feeling like the smartest one in the room** because, well, this was a book she knew inside and out – she knew it word for word! When the teacher got to the page talking about the heavy construction equipment, she asked, "Does anyone know what this is?"

Sarah's hand shot up. She practically came out of her chair with enthusiasm. The teacher called on Sarah, who proudly answered, "It's a Snort!" Everyone laughed, including the teacher. It wasn't a mean, *laughing-at-Sarah* sort of laugh. They thought she was making a joke. Sarah laughed too, hoping to play along and carry out the charade.

In her mind, however, she decided every single person in that room was smarter than she was. She realized her classmates knew it wasn't really called a Snort – that's what the baby bird called it. *Everyone* knew that except for her. For the rest of Sarah's school days and for years after, she always thought, *"Everyone in this room is smarter than I am, and I was found out!"*

She thought that by succeeding in her business she would end this constant battle in her soul. She never was *dumb*, but she didn't have the brain "equipment" to understand that, as a child. **This lie was embedded and solidified over the years** and there was nothing she could do, externally, now, to prove it wrong.

My *Fight*

When my awareness of these things started, I noticed that my need was not just to be *special* – I needed to be the **most** *special*. It was an insatiable craving that drove me, unconsciously, at every moment. The ironic thing is that I could never be *special* enough. I was trying to heal an internal wound with external Band-Aids. As it is for anything internal, there will never be enough external validation.

Along with the no-rhyme-or-reason aspect, my need to be *special* didn't involve **everything** in my life. It was just in the things that mattered to me. I'd explain this, but it was decided without logic, so therefore explaining it to your logical brain would sound crazy. It even sounds crazy to me as I write this; but the need to be *special* in areas the monster had me convinced were necessary, consumed me. My need shaped my social interactions, my relationships, and my self-image.

The danger of this toxic wiring is that I could never fully have a relationship with anyone else. It was always about me. Oh, and did I mention me? And then there's always **me, me, and me!**

Mary Kay Ash, the founder of Mary Kay Cosmetics, has a notable quote I have long believed. She says, "Imagine everyone you meet has a sign around their neck that says, 'Make me feel important.'" And this bit of brilliance is not new. Dale Carnegie's classic *How to Win Friends and Influence People* teaches this powerful principle as well. I wanted to live my life by these principles, but the lie I had operated under for so long made it impossible for me to make anyone else feel important when I was so busy making sure they knew how *special* I was.

Luckily these patterns emerged when I was able to observe them. I started to see the dysfunctional relationships left in my wake in trying to be *special*. Add to that the fact I never felt *special* ENOUGH no matter how hard I tried. That is the juncture where I finally started investigating these principles.

> **NOTE:**
>
> We never really have a relationship with anyone else other than ourselves. When we are consumed emotionally by keeping up the façade – **fearing** or **proving** our monster's lie – we can't *fully* give ourselves to others in our most important relationships. We can't truly hear another person.

Now that I know how to recognize these patterns, I see them all around me. People compensate for their own personal lie in an attempt to ensure that others will like them and think they are smart, perfect, capable, relevant, and worthwhile. People play either the - I am okay and let me make sure you know it or the I hope no one finds out what a real loser I really am - card.

Recently I've even heard of a condition called the **"Imposter Syndrome"** where someone can't internalize or acknowledge their accomplishments. They feel like an "imposter." Sounds like their monster has done a great job convincing them of what a loser they are. And this is a great example of what it feels like.

My *Flight*

I was in the process of writing this book when I attended my company's leadership event. I have been a trainer and speaker in my company, but the last few years I've been semi-retired and not up in front speaking and training as much as I was in the past. I was dreading attending this yearly event because many people knew I was writing this book, and I knew people would be asking about it. *I was completely shut down in my writing at this time,* and I felt myself just **wanting to hide**.

Ironically, many people approached me to say how much my training and speaking had meant to them over the years. Many told me they missed me and even recounted specific training or talks I had given that had ended up being a turning point in their business or life. The stories being told to me were incredible and so monumental. The *special* Kim should have been in heaven!

But what I noticed was, I became increasingly uncomfortable. I felt myself **shrinking back.** I was not enjoying it. I felt myself wanting to run and hide. I didn't want any more people telling me how wonderful I was! The more that people complimented me, the more I felt like a phony. I had the "Imposter Syndrome" *feeling* to the max. **I felt shame.**

I've learned to observe my reactions and not believe them, so I went back to my room to process my feelings and thoughts. I called my son, Kris. He has done a fair amount of his own monster work and is a good sounding board for me.

He told me, "Mom! You just got bit by the *flight* message. Both the *fight* (to prove you are *special*) and the *flight* (believing you are not *special*) are responses to the same lie. *Special* is the illusory antidote you never needed." **(Oh, you sneaky monster, you!)**

Our Identity

With this monster process, many of us have developed fantastic skills! I **had** to be *special*, so, in addition to achieving the highest ranks within my profession, I can play the piano and sing while doing it; I can direct teams of people in business, theater, and music; I am an entrepreneur; I have thrived on making my own way. I am thankful for my success and my skills. The skills I developed aren't going away if I de-fang the monster. The important difference is the energy source these skills originate from (I'll discuss this more in chapter 7).

At one of my events, Melanie, a successful business client of mine, was asked what she would be without her monster. She said, "Without my monster, I'd be a slob sitting on my sofa, watching TV all day, eating bon-bons. I need my monster to succeed."

She knew that she was being driven by monster energy. (Not to be confused with the sports drink!) She was self-aware enough to also know that it wasn't healthy for her. She feared that if she discovered and uncovered her monster, she would be a failure in her business and therefore in her life – even though it was running her ragged. She was never happy, because she could not be successful *enough*. Her assumption was that she wouldn't be successful without *fight* energy.

> There is a part of us that fears if the monster is proven illusory, the survival mechanisms we have developed will also go away, and therefore who will we be?

At the same event, Annie, another attendee and I, were chatting about these monster concepts.

She stopped the conversation and grabbed my arm and said, "Kim, you better not tell me there isn't a monster under there. I will **not** be happy!"

"Why?" I asked.

"If there wasn't a monster to point to – to have as the backdrop of all the decisions, mistakes, problems, conflicts, and beliefs in my life – then everything in my life has been built on a lie."

And there you have the crux of it. So much of our identity is built around that original lie and its subsequent survival mechanisms. These are two great examples of both sides of the lie. Melanie, whose success is tied to the *fight* strategy, and Annie who stays in *flight* mode and needs the monster to justify her failures.

There is a part of us that fears if the monster is proven illusory, the survival mechanisms we have developed will also go away, and therefore who will we be? What part of our identity will be at risk if we lift the bedspread to see there isn't really a monster at all? And, what familiar, but dysfunctional, benefits are we getting by keeping the lie alive?

The purpose of this process is to observe the way the monster has been driving our thoughts, actions and identity *our entire life*. Now, with the amazing prefrontal part of our brain, we can look at our old wiring and make new pathways. Once we look at this process critically and understand what drives us, we can stop the craziness of reacting and lovingly take the frightened four-year-old out of the driver's seat.

Chapter 3

How the Monster "Roars"

Since some of these survival mechanisms can be beneficial on one hand, on the other hand, it can be difficult to tell which thoughts are coming from the monster or which are coming from our authentic self. It is important to know the difference. But how can one tell when the monster is triggered? The first place I look is how I am feeling. When I *feel* fear, stress, anxiety, panic, any un-ease, I *will* hear the monster's voice – that's what I call **chatter**.

Chatter encompasses all the destructive and non-serving words, phrases, and meanings running through our minds. Chatter sounds like it's coming from us. It speaks in our voice. It knows our logic, it has read all the books we have read, and attended all the same seminars. It is a part of us and probably knows more about us, subconsciously, than we do.

Aligning or Observing

We rarely take the time to **observe** and investigate the thoughts streaming in our mind. We just hear them, think they must be true, and then we respond to whatever the message is. This is what I refer to as *aligning with the thought*. The "GPS" to help us determine if we have aligned with our negative chatter or not, are our emotions.

It's natural to align with the voice in our head. It's the same stream of thoughts running through our minds telling us why we can't, why we *shouldn't*, or why we've never been able to (*flight*). Or, it's telling us that we *have* to win, be perfect, work harder, or be the best (*fight*). We know we've triggered the monster when our thoughts are saying these things, which immediately lead to negative emotions. This is what I refer to as having a **monster mindset.**

Several years ago, I had a coaching conversation with Sharon, one of my team leaders, regarding her business. In discussing some of her struggles, she claimed she didn't have any chatter.

To this I said, "Really? Wow. That would be amazing if you didn't."

Moments prior she had recounted to me how worried she was about her business numbers going down. She gave me her stats saying, "**These are the numbers, and they don't lie.**"

She went on to interpret the data – or I should say: Her monster interpreted the data. She sadly concluded, "Kim, I don't think I can do this business anymore. I guess I'm not a good leader. So many people on my team have quit. I know that's why my business is tanking."

"Sharon, do you hear it?", I asked. "Do you hear the chatter?"

"It's not chatter, Kim. It's the **truth.**"

I said, "Sharon, businesses ebb and flow. That's all it means. I have people quit regularly, too."

"No, I can't do this." She mentioned another team leader. "John's business is thriving. People are flocking to join him. I just don't have it, and I know that's why my business is going down so fast."

"Okay, Sharon...you have to hear that, right? Hear the chatter?"

"Kim! It's not chatter! It's the truth!"

On and on we discussed, and on and on she defended her *truth* - aka **aligned** *with the thought*. She didn't **hear** these thoughts as chatter, but emotionally she felt defeated and distressed.

She thought about our conversation that evening. She told me the next day about a conversation in her head that went something like this: *"You're just a big phony."* To this she vehemently responded, *"No! I was never phony. I believed what I said when I said it. I never lied or led anyone falsely."*

As she finished defending herself, it dawned on her to ask herself, *"Who am I talking to?"* It was the same voice in her head that had told her the **truth** earlier. She moved to *observing the thought* - instead of *aligning with it*. She separated out the voice and saw it for what it was: Chatter. *VOILA!*

The numbers on paper reflected a downward cycle; that's just data. When that data touches the lie inside us - *I'm not good enough, I suck!* - The monster is triggered and proceeds to give us the *meaning* of the data. Chatter will make sure we know why it happened and the role we played in it – usually, how inadequate we are. **This**

happens in a nanosecond in our mind and we usually aren't even aware of it.

Even while I write this chapter about chatter, I find myself riddled with it. As an example of how this plays out, I will detail what *my* chatter is saying right at this moment:

"Kim, you're a nobody! You don't even have a college degree. What makes you think you can talk about how the brain works? You aren't qualified in any way. You should really just "stay in your lane." You're a speaker. You're not a writer. And you know what? The world doesn't really need another "self-help" book anyway. Look at all the books out there. You aren't saying anything new. It's all been said before. You aren't going to be able to compete with all the amazing people out there already. Just stop. Go back to enjoying your life."

Do you get a sense of this voice? Can you feel the emotion I am potentially feeling as I write this?

Let's examine it: Is there any truth in my chatter's message? **Absolutely!**

The facts are:

- I don't have a college degree.
- I've never written a book before.
- I identify more as a speaker than as a writer.
- There are a *ton* of self-help books on the market.
- I am probably not saying anything brand new or that hasn't been discussed before.

But just like in the example of Sharon's business numbers, the **rub** is in the interpretation I allow chatter to decide about *me*. Chatter will take the facts, but all I will hear will be the message of one of the three F's.

- **Flight** – *I am not good enough to write this book...*
- **Fight** – *Oh yeah! Watch me! I'll show you!*
- **Freeze** – *Um, I need to think about this more. I'll get to it soon. Really.*

If I **aligned** with this chatter, I would stop writing right now. The only reason I'm still typing this paragraph, and beyond, is that I *know* what chatter sounds and *feels* like. I have learned to shift to the **observer** of these thoughts, as opposed to *aligning* with them, as quickly as I can. This entire book process is a scary one for me; it's way out of my comfort zone and it definitely breaks the status quo. It's taken me longer than I thought, because of the influence of chatter; but since I knew it was chatter, I knew it wouldn't ultimately stop me.

Chatter Creation

Identifying chatter is one of the most difficult and important aspects of this entire process. Our monster is just doing what it has always done: Keeping us from looking "under the bed" – where the lie lives!

It remembers the *fearful feeling* your illogical 4-year-old-self felt, and although it has ZERO understanding why you felt that way, *it doesn't want you to feel that way again.* These thoughts continue producing similar emotions, which create more chatter thoughts, which exacerbate the, already negative, emotions. And the cycle continues. ***These thoughts and emotions go hand in hand.*** This is where it all started.

Can you see why sometimes when you're in a funk, or even in deep despair, it can just get worse and worse? It feels like a downward spiral that picks up speed as it goes. Now you see why.

Have you heard the saying "What you think about, comes about"? In an insightful article entitled "Don't Believe Everything You Think," the Cleveland Clinic Wellness program claims, "Each person has an average of 60,000 thoughts a day! That's one thought per second in every waking hour! Amazingly, 95 percent are the same thoughts repeated every day. On average, 80 percent of those habitual thoughts are negative." These negative thoughts are what I'm calling chatter; thoughts that **initiated from the lie** and lead to a *flight, fight* or *freeze* message.

Neurons that fire together - wire together.

This is why paying attention to what you're thinking about is so worth the effort. I referred earlier to Hebb's Law, "*Neurons that fire together - wire together.*" There are two main factors that contribute to this firing and wiring process:

Firing - The strength of the emotion felt

Wiring - How many times that emotion is repeated

This has created our thought/feeling loop. As you can see, this process has resulted in neurological pathways being created and embedded over the years with the monster driving. In a nano-second, our lie can be threatened, resulting in a triggered Amy who has one of the *flight, fight* or *freeze* messages at the ready. The grooves of these *response thoughts* have **muscle memory** and we act accordingly and automatically. According to neuroscientists, our behavior is only 5 percent conscious, and the other 95 percent is unconscious. Our reality is primarily created by our unconscious thoughts which, in turn, were created from this firing and wiring process.

A conscious thought happens when you're focused on something specific like deciding what color to paint your living room or following directions for the first time. When you learned to tie your shoes, you needed to think about each step; but once it was learned, it becomes established thought wiring; or an unconscious thought. This can be helpful, but it can also establish habits we wish we didn't have. We can get up in the morning, shower, drive to work, work all day, drive home, make dinner, surf Facebook, kick back, and watch TV while only using 5 percent of our conscious mind all day long. This doesn't lead to a fulfilled life, but it feels familiar and safe.

What Triggers Chatter?

Our monster loves the **status quo**. If you approach your habits with any apprehension, worry, fear or judgment, you will trigger the monster and hear chatter. If you approach the new thing you are attempting neutrally, or with excitement and anticipation, it may not trigger;

but fear and excitement process similarly in the body. If your mind stays in the **"happy place,"** the monster will not awaken.

The point of this principle is that how you approach something is critical to its effect on you. What runs in the backdrop of all thought, emotion, and action is the *feeling* or assumptions you have about the thing you are attempting.

I have long admired the teaching of Kelly McGonigal. In her seminal book *The Willpower Instinct* – as well as in talks she has given to professional organizations – she has referenced how dangerous stress is, and the role it played in mortality studies. I was surprised to find a more recent TED Talk where she basically repented and recanted her findings regarding stress.

She has a new book out, *The Upside of Stress*, where she re-examines her studies on stress to uncover some surprising findings. She recently discovered that it wasn't *stress* that killed people, but that stress is only destructive to those who *interpret* stress as bad or who **believe** stress will kill them.

In regard to engaging with your monster, McGonigal's conclusions directly apply. *How* you approach something and how you *feel* about something is one of the biggest indicators of how it will effect on you. The belief or **mindset**, when approaching anything, will determine the ultimate, long-term effect it will have on you.

Remember in my story, earlier, where I attended the leadership event and felt the *flight* message? When I analyzed that deeper, I realized that the *monster mindset* was in full force, at that time, regarding me and my abilities. I felt overwhelmed, defeated, tired, and hopeless in regard to this book. I attended that event with *flight energy* running my *emotional operating system.* The stories people were sharing with me about the impact I had made on them over the years, actually exacerbated the pain. My "ears" were aligned with the *flight chatter*, and it didn't matter that the two events were completely unrelated. **The monster was in control** of how I heard and saw everything else in my life, at that time.

Many times, we approach something new with apprehension and fear. That's a sure way to trigger chatter. If you attempt doing something you've failed at previously, or you have a strong reason to believe you will fail this time, be prepared to hear a cacophony of chatter. Remember, **chatter is your voice** telling you things that you experienced in the past. Its loudness will be commensurate with the degree of shame/blame/guilt/fear - aka negative **emotions,** you've associated with it.

Several years ago, with the acceleration of

> **If you attempt doing something you've failed at previously, or you have a strong reason to believe you will fail this time, be prepared to hear a cacophony of chatter.**

technology, my 80-year-old mother-in-law, Susan, was attempting to learn how to work the computer. She was excited about the possibilities it afforded her, but she continued to feel overwhelmed by all the new things she needed to learn. Things like attaching a file, copying and pasting, or opening a new browser window, for example, would send her into a panic.

One day as she was lamenting her inadequacy, I had her do an experiment. First, I had her take a deep breath and, while she was breathing, say in her mind, **"This is easy,"** over and over. Every time she sat down at the computer, she would follow this pattern. In fact, I think she even got the Staples "Easy Button" as a visual to put beside her computer.

Over time, she became excited about learning new tricks and strategies on the computer. The benefit of learning technology overrode, emotionally, the learning curve she would need to experience. The **"juice was worth the squeeze"**, so to speak. She is a pro today, whereas I know many older people who won't participate in the technology age. They stayed in their *this is hard* mindset. Therefore, new things will always be overwhelming, hard, and un-learnable.

Stop the Fight

One of the biggest secrets I've learned in dealing with the monster and its incessant chatter is that you cannot fight with it! You cannot overcome it. And you cannot argue with it. When we fight or resist, we create more fear, stress, and anxiety inside ourselves. And because Amy responds to **how we feel** to begin with, this is a futile cycle. The more we fight it, the more fuel we are throwing on the monster's fire.

Remember, that part of our brain still does not have a logical connection. Amy only *feels* your fear/stress/ anxiety, assumes the worst, gives you one of the F's it is conditioned to give, and stands at the ready. It stays on **high alert** to save you from the possible death that must be near – why else would you *feel* this way? You can see how this quickly becomes a fight you will never win and one that can lead to serious problems as a result.

In Elizabeth Gilbert's book *Big Magic*, she talks about how she handles her monster, which she refers to as fear. She learned that fear will always be a presence in her life if she wants to create. In order for her to have her genius, inevitably apprehension will be sparked in her. It is in these moments, the instances where greatness is at stake, she will hear chatter the most.

In her book, Gilbert shares her strategy for dealing with this aspect of creation. She likens her relationship to fear to that of taking a **road trip** with a long-time friend. She knows her monster is her companion for the entire trip. Instead of attempting to kick it to the curb when it gets mouthy, Gilbert talks to her monster and says, kindly, "Fear, you will have a voice in my life and will always be allowed to go with me, but you will sit in the back seat and can **NOT** touch any of the dials."

This is a perfect *mindset* example and one that will serve us well. She felt fear but is *not afraid of the fear*. She does not despise it, resist it, judge it, or hate it. Rather, she sees it as necessary for creation. It rides along with her and always will. Any time she ventures into the world of creation, fear will be there. *She does not try to fight the fear.*

Gilbert is able to approach her fear with calm, **loving energy**; an observer, if you will. It's like dealing with a child. We love them, but they don't have the understanding of what's happening. You wouldn't let them drive, but also you wouldn't exhaust yourself trying to help them understand.

Dieting and Chatter

From experiences in my health business, I've seen chatter thrive in the dieter, because dieting many times begins from the lie that you are not good, worthy, or perfect, *enough*. The message is: *"You HAVE to look good, be skinny, or be beautiful, to be loveable."* One look at the magazine covers at the checkout stand will show you how the monster is driving that message. It starts young.

I'll list many of the perspectives I've heard repeated to me regarding this topic in my decade (plus) time as a health and weight loss coach. I would guess your chatter has said something similar. If your struggle is not with dieting, look at these as possible examples of chatter that can be applied to your specific situation.

The chatter says, If I don't lose weight, aren't skinny, don't look perfect, (fill in the blank):

- I will lose all control of my life.
- My spouse won't love me anymore.
- I won't look good in a swimsuit.
- I'll be judged by others
- I'll get stretch marks

The ultimate conclusion, *emotionally*, is **I'm NOT ACCEPTABLE!**

Chatter helps us, through *flight* messages with the reasons we can't do what we want, as well:
- I can't afford a gym membership.
- I don't have time to go to the gym.
- I can't afford to eat well.
- I have never been able to keep weight off.
- I've always been fat.
- I can't really do this long term.
- I can't exercise anyway (for a variety of reasons), so I can't be healthy.
- I'm not a good cook, so I have to eat crappy food.
- I'm going to start on Monday.
- I'm going to start tomorrow, REALLY!
- I can't eat healthily with my travel schedule.
- I am bad.
- I cheated.
- I need an accountability group or partner.
- I need a better health coach, diet program, gym, house, water bottle.
- I should know better.
- I have no willpower!

Whatever your specific issue, remember chatter can get rather ludicrous. When fear, stress, and apprehension are involved, the amygdala has no choice but to respond with survival strategies, which will include one of the three F's. Chatter is how we hear those messages.

It is important to remember that when it comes to *survival*, Amy is specifically wired. Survival includes food and procreation. When Amy senses anxiety, one of its strongest illogical messages will be to **eat**. (You will need to *live* to be able to have sex, so eating comes first!)

The *Monster Mindset*

When I first lost weight with the program my health company offers, it was with little belief or trust that it would work for me. I had tried so many other programs before, that I went into this one with more of "I'll try it and see" energy. I didn't have shame regarding my body, my husband loved me no matter what and I wasn't driven by perfectionism or Madison Avenue propaganda. I just wanted to feel better and overcome the *feeling* of being a food addict. (I wasn't a food addict, but some days I felt like it!)

Because I had a calm, hopeful, mindset going into this program, I was surprised to find myself dropping weight quickly. The first week of any new eating program can be exciting, but more exciting for me was how my cravings were affected. It was a miracle! I was happy, thankful, and **ecstatic** about everything that was happening.

Do you think I heard any chatter at this point? Nope - not a word.

The program, which starts with a weight loss plan, is very structured and the food is supplied, so it was easy. I was never tempted- **in the least** - to eat anything else. I faced pizza, cookies, chips, my normal nemeses, with **ZERO** temptation!

But when my involvement with this company shifted to actually *helping others*, they started referring to me as a "health coach". They even started paying me - *very* well! This caused some *monster emotions* to be triggered, especially when I started struggling. When the scale would vacillate a little - fear kicked in. I felt panic that I had just fooled myself and the weight was coming back. The *feeling* that now people were relying on me, the pressure I felt from that, also that people were judging me, (real or perceived), guilt, shame, and lack of integrity started to brew inside me.

Did I hear chatter at this point? **Absolutely!**

When attempting to go back on the weight loss phase of the program, with the *monster mindset* I was in, temptations were everywhere. Willpower is not sustainable, so I found myself regularly giving into the temptations. I had "*day one*," again and again.

This behavior created more guilt and shame, which was accompanied by more chatter. We feel the initial fear, and as it starts compounding with the other emotions, we get caught in a downward emotional spiral. We keep eating to feel better, which leads to us just feeling *worse*.

It starts with the *monster mindset* during the approach. This is a major contributor to why dieters get caught in this unhealthy loop. Did you know one of the biggest factors of weight gain is DIETING? Just like my mother-in-law's experience with technology, how something is approached emotionally, is a determining factor, of its success, long-term.

For those who eat to make themselves feel better, (which is most people, to some degree) many can find themselves in the diet/binge yo-yo cycle. Amy doesn't know that you weigh 300 pounds and have diabetes, and that there is a plethora of accessible food. It only knows and obeys the *emotions of fear*. It wants you to *feel* better! Eating is one way to accomplish that – at least until the shame sets in, and that's when the trouble compounds.

I've also known people who don't get hungry in times of stress. In fact, they don't want to eat at all. They have no appetite for food. The negative emotions are still there, however. These people can easily turn to other numbing substances – alcohol, drugs, pornography, shopping, video games, and TV, to name a few. They don't usually struggle with obesity; but Amy is still committed to their **emotional pain relief.** I will address compulsions and addictions later in the book, but chatter is a strong factor in this discussion.

My successful business client, Melanie who worried about becoming a lazy couch potato, was living in such fear of being worthless; she **had** to be successful in her business. Her monster stayed triggered, and chatter commenced. In fact, her chatter had created her thought wiring and served to drive the lie deeper and deeper. She kept hearing the message *Work harder, longer, more intense. Don't stop! If you slow down, you know what will happen?*

Here's a quick test: How many of you are hearing chatter right now in your thoughts? Are you feeling fearful about what I'm talking about? Are you feeling apprehension? Do you feel kind of sick to your stomach? Is your heart beating faster while you've been reading this? Then you are hearing chatter – 100 percent guaranteed!

If you can, stop and listen to it. *Be an observer.* It may be saying, *"Don't listen to this crazy woman! You don't want to look at this. You know what will happen if you do! You know what people will think if they find out the truth about you!"*

Awareness is the biggest part of this process. It creates a path from autopilot to choice. Once we know and can engage our awesome prefrontal cortex – the thinking counterpart to Amy's illogical reactions – then we will have tools to prepare for, identify, and deal with chatter. We can, then, choose what serves us best in our lives. It's true freedom!

> **Awareness is the biggest part of this process. It creates a path from autopilot to choice.**

Chapter 4

The RAS

"When we change the way we look at things,
the things we look at change."
– Wayne Dyer

There is an interesting gatekeeper living in our brain called the Reticular Activating System (RAS). One of its purposes is to manage and monitor what information gets our attention. This is a critical process our brain has developed. If we needed to manage and deal with every bit of stimuli that hit our senses every second of every minute, of every hour, of every day, we would explode! The RAS's job is to ensure that we only receive the data that we need to survive – or that we've given significance to. So, part of its function is instinctual, and part of it is conditioned.

The instinctual part of the RAS knows to be aware of where food is, for example – so you won't starve. It also pays very close attention to the person with whom you may discover "chemistry." It **wakes up** when you feel that *certain vibe*, and it is watching, making sure you are on full love alert. This is our sex instinct, and the RAS turns up the dials on *that data reception instantly*. It makes sure you notice the look, the tone of voice, the fact that they did or didn't call when they said they would, or that you hear their ringtone from the phone buried deep in your purse.

I remember my first love and how my radar was running full force for anything that had to do with him. He drove a silver Toyota truck. And while I had never paid attention to those vehicles before, once my RAS had been activated, I noticed every silver Toyota truck - **all of the time.** *It could be him!*

In fact, speaking of noticing cars – this would fall under conditioned awareness of our RAS. Think about the last time you went car shopping. You did your research, and you decided that the car for you was, let's say, a red VW Jetta. Did you notice how many red VW Jettas there were all of a sudden? They are on TV commercials, in the parking lots, and in front of you in traffic. Everywhere! Is it possible that the entire world decided to buy a red VW Jetta at the same time you did?

The truth is those cars have been there all along, but their significance wasn't programmed into your brain. You didn't notice them before. That is your RAS at work. Its job is to only let you see what you've communicated, through emotion, is important to you. And while you are noticing all the red VW Jettas around you, your RAS does not point out to you the plethora of black Hondas – that is, until you want one. Then, when you want a black Honda, watch them multiply.

Another example of a conditioned response is how my RAS notices specific times. My anniversary is Nov. 11, so I swear that every time I look at a clock, it always displays 11:11. Or another time that I give significance to is 12:34. I used to think it was a cosmic message that the universe was communicating to me, but then I became aware of this part of our brain. In reality, I looked at the clock many more times a day than those times, but I didn't notice it. It had no significance, so the RAS didn't let that information get my attention.

Our brains adapt to every situation, and what is experienced, with strong emotion, gets the attention of the RAS. A mother who slept as hard as a rock prior to having a baby becomes the lightest sleeper, and hears every whimper during the night. And later, during the child's teen years, while waiting and worrying when her child will get home, she

> **Our brains adapt to every situation, and what is experienced, with strong emotion, gets the attention of the RAS.**

85

hears every car and car door slam. Her RAS is on high alert because of the emotional significance she gives the subject.

Additionally, because our thoughts are steered by neural pathways created previously, we typically notice only the *truth* of what we already believe. It's called a *confirmation bias.* This falls into the habit of thought we discussed in the chatter chapter. We see what we've always seen and hear what we've always heard.

When we were young, we embedded, with emotion, the lie; that we aren't *good enough* or that we are *unworthy* and *unacceptable.* So, without questioning, the RAS only lets in the data supporting that truth. It doesn't question what it's been told.

This was precisely the case with me and my needing to be *special.* I would find myself locking in on people I perceived to have the *special sauce* I needed. These people were the most *special.* (My sister, Kathi and my friend Kathy Paul, for example) Sometimes I hated them, and sometimes, I wanted what they had so badly, I would **imitate** them. My RAS would make me acutely aware of all their *specialness,* and then chatter sometimes gave me the *flight* message *I'm so average - not special, not ok.* Many times, that would lead straight to the *fight* message *Oh yeah! Watch this!* to prove how *special* I was.

In my business career, I spent many years worrying about how I was being perceived. Of course, my monster wanted everyone to realize how *special* I *really* was. The RAS was on guard to show me any **hint** of my not being *special* enough. It interpreted comments, jokes, glances, non-glances, as not being *special* enough. The thought that there was another explanation for people's behavior never occurred to that part of me, the *having-to-be-special* Kim. The RAS was there to make sure I saw and interpreted exactly how I had programmed it.

> **Note:**
>
> If we only realized how little people actually thought about us, this wouldn't take up nearly as much mental energy! They are all busy hiding and proving their own lie - they could care less about ours! Oh, what needless pain we bear when we worry about what people think of us.

Mental Bloodhounds

Our RAS are like "Mental Bloodhounds" because that is what it does. The original, emotional lie, dressed up like the truth, is given by the monster to the bloodhounds. (Think: dirty socks!) That puts the bloodhounds on the hunt for any supporting evidence to prove *only* what it was told: the lie! The monster, through chatter, will make sure it does.

Throughout our lives, this is what keeps the lie alive *under the bed*. The bloodhounds have been trained and will always find evidence of **why** *I'm not okay* or that *I'm only average*. This sparks the monster anew and keeps me in *flight, fight,* or *freeze* mode - and the **cycle continues.**

The role of these mental bloodhounds **cannot** be diminished. If not for this feature, we would have probably forgotten, or overridden the original lie as we developed more cognitive understanding. However, our unconscious minds are not naturally connected to time or logic. *We believe anything processed with strong emotion as true; even if from a four-year-old.* (Fire and Wire - remember?) and unless there are new emotional pathways to rethink and rewire our interpretations, we are still the four-year-old wondering if we are okay.

Viola and Ruth

Growing up, we had a family friend who would visit occasionally. Her name was Viola. "Viola, I sure appreciate you," my mom said one evening after dinner. "Thanks for helping me clean up the kitchen. I love having you around. You are such a help."

Viola beamed back. "I know. Everybody wants me around. Everybody loves me."

Viola was childlike. She was always so cheerful and helpful. She would help clear the table after dinner and just hang out in the kitchen to help and visit with whoever else was working.

This particular story was repeated to me often by my mom as I grew up. It made a huge impression on her. Viola already knew people loved her – she wasn't looking for confirmation of this; it was a given fact! Anything that happened to her in the real world just confirmed the **truth** of this: "Everybody loves me and wants me around."

Her bloodhounds always brought her evidence of how people loved her and how people wanted to have her around. She never had a thought that she was a bother, and interestingly enough, she was right. People loved having her around.

Contrast Viola's story with the following story of Ruth. I grew up in church, usually singing in one form or another. This particular Sunday, as usual, I was in the choir. The choir seats were on the platform facing the audience.

One Sunday, after the offering was taken, the ushers came forward and the pastor prayed over it. Afterward, while singing a song, the ushers took the offering baskets out to an office somewhere. The congregation then greeted each other and sat back down.

Brother Jones was the head usher. He was a prominent banker in our town and was ultra-proper, rich, and usually cranky – or so my middle school friends and I thought. He had gathered all the offering baskets and was taking them out the back door to the church office, when he did something that none of us had ever seen or expected: **He skipped!** He was smiling and skipping all across the back of the church. The congregation was not aware. Only the people on the platform could see this.

My friends and I looked at each other amid giggles and nudges everywhere. Luckily, this was while people greeted each other across pews and the aisle, so our behavior wasn't altogether inappropriate. We were reacting to Brother Jones, and we weren't thinking anyone in particular was noticing us.

This is where Ruth comes in. After the service was over about 30 minutes later, everyone stood to exit the chapel. The choir was coming down from the platform, and I gathered with my normal group of friends – because that's what kids in middle school do. All of a sudden, Ruth, who had gone against the exiting sea of people to find her way to me and my friends, came up red-faced to talk to us.

She said, "I saw you."

We looked at each other, confused.

She continued. "I saw you laughing up there."

We looked more confused. The Brother Jones incident felt like a long time ago at that point. We'd forgotten about it with this angry woman confronting us now.

"I know why you were laughing," she said. "You saw me pull down my girdle! I think that was very rude of you and you ought to be ashamed." And then she stormed off. Well, you know what my friends and I did, of course. We laughed at her - behind her back.

She knew – she was certain – it was *her* we were laughing at while she adjusted her girdle.[1] There was no convincing her otherwise. Her bloodhounds, doing their job, proved her right. I can't say for sure, but she probably was on high alert, *in life*, for people making fun of her and/or not liking her. Seeing us laugh at the same time she pulled on her girdle to sit down meant, *no doubt*, we were laughing and making fun of her. To her, we were rude and should be ashamed.

> **Our interpretations about ourselves will dictate how we see everything in life.**

Viola and Ruth are at opposite ends of the spectrum. Most people fall in the middle somewhere, but the reality of this principle plays out continually in our lives.

---

[1] Girdle - an old-fashioned version of Spanks

Our interpretations about ourselves will dictate how we see everything in life. The ridiculing teenagers pushed that button for Ruth, and an offense was taken where none was given. Such is how it goes. The bloodhounds will show us what we have told it is true. The knee-jerk reactions from these interpretations about ourselves will decide how we interpret all situations in which we find ourselves.

Viola: *Everyone loves me.*
Why wouldn't they?
Ruth: *Everyone laughs at me.*
Why wouldn't they?

Our *truth* is decided and embedded by our young, illogical selves. If any situation matches our predominate belief, that information is let in. If it contradicts our predominate belief, we won't notice it. That's the mental bloodhound's job.

This also holds true for what we believe about others. If we believe our spouse is a slob, we will notice only the times they leave their dirty clothes on the floor. We won't notice the times they pick up their clothes. Our labels can keep people locked in the *truth* that doesn't serve them or us. As long as we see them that way, not only could it be a case of our **not** seeing contrary evidence that is there; but they could feel this *truth* emanating from us, sub-verbally, and be discouraged from changing.

Here are some examples:

"Oh, my son – he is so rebellious."

"My daughter – she is so mouthy!"

"My boss is a jerk. He treats me like crap."

"My mother-in-law is such a control freak."

This relates back to the Wayne Dyer quote at the beginning of the chapter. "When you change the way you look at things, the things you look at change." When we give a new *truth* to our bloodhounds, the evidence shift is amazing. You will start noticing things that you never have noticed before, just like the example of the red VW Jetta. Everything in your world will shift. You will feel lighter and happier when you come from a new *truth*.

What would happen if you started seeing yourself with a new truth – that you are unconditionally loved and worthy? What if you were to reprogram your early wiring with this message? Chatter won't let that happen easily, but remember, don't fight your way to this *truth*. I will share how to rewire in chapter 8; but there is a way, and it can start now.

It starts by looking to find the *truth* that you are intrinsically and unconditionally loved. Look at yourself like you are four years old again. Would you love your four-year-old self? This is an extremely emotional process, as it needs to be, to accomplish new "firing", but remember, **that's who needs your love now.**

Chapter 5

The Monster Tracks

Most people can identify their monster by noticing how they react to given situations. I call these reactions *monster tracks*. The best way we can truly know what is driving us, is to observe and notice our reactions. If we only listen to our thoughts, we will stay aligned with them, and, as a result, trapped in the same thinking our young self created. Our thoughts – a.k.a. chatter – will **always** justify and rationalize our response.

We can gauge if our reactions are of the monster variety, primarily by the energy we feel. The feelings include,

> **The best way we can truly know what is driving us, is to observe and notice our reactions.**

but aren't limited to, panic, mania, and intense urgency. It's a sensation of being **driven**.

These tracks are our go-to reactions. They are the first signal, for most of us, of the monster hiding under our bed. Without this context, these tracks will just be dismissed as:

- Who we are,
- Our upbringing
- Part of life
- Understandable *given my situation*

Let's recap the process:

A. Illogical thoughts (the only kind we have access to early in life) led to the illogical emotions of fear of not being acceptable in our community. (The lie - aka the monster)

B. This fear triggered our survival brain (Amy), who answers with only one of these messages: *flight, fight,* or *freeze*.

C. We continue to see **only** the evidence of what our inaccurate and illogical emotions have told our bloodhounds is *true*. Evidences start showing up as we grow; *proving to us the truthfulness of the lie*, which continues to trigger the monster anew.

D. From Amy's responses, we have developed strengths and skills that have largely created our identity, *for the negative and the positive.* Not only do we shy away from things we may not be good at (*flight*), but we also produced skills and talents in order to prove our worth (*fight*) **All of it creates our identity**.

The continued practice of this process over time has laid down a neurological pathway in our psyche. As we grow, we continue to build on this illogical foundation of thought and feelings. This is why our reactions feel so justified. They are **familiar**. They are deep inside us and like the grooves in a road, they pull us back into them without our awareness.

With this process running in the background, we add our family's influence. We watch our parents to see what they think, how they react to situations, and what they value. We take our clues from them, and these become the *truth* that we either adopt in our young age, or react against in adolescence. Either way, it is based on an illogical, monster-driven premise. We therefore have little hope of thinking and feeling anything different than what was created by our illogical and "half-brained" little selves.

Can you see why noticing our monster tracks (our reactions) can be an effective way of revealing where our monster is lurking?

I like the visual example of the original lie being the hub of a wheel and the monster tracks as the spokes leading to it. As you deal with releasing a spoke (one of the tracks), you can find some immediate relief in your heart and life.

This is why we want to pay attention to these monster tracks and see if we can release them. Even releasing one spoke can create powerful momentum toward running to the roar and uncovering the lie.

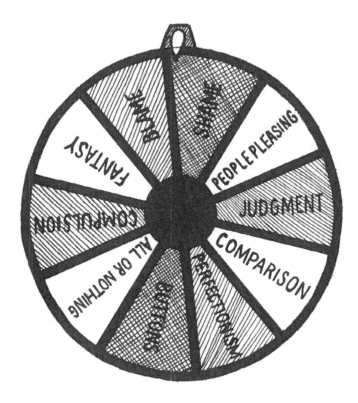

Here is an overview of the monster tracks. There are more reactions that can be included, but these are the ten I identified, first.

1. Shame - Feelings of having to live in hiding because of personal secrets.
2. People Pleasing - Being driven to do what others want rather than what you want.
3. Judgment – Thinking in terms of RIGHT/WRONG, BLACK/WHITE, AGREE/DISAGREE.
4. Comparison – Comparing your life to others'.
5. Perfectionism – Feeling determined to do things perfectly.

6. Buttons – Taking things personally or being easily angered.
7. All or Nothing – Thinking in "either/or" instead of "and/both" terms.
8. Compulsion – Feeling out of control in certain behaviors.
9. Fantasy – If only _____, then you'd be happy.
10. Blame – Looking to an external reason for your problems.

As we discuss each monster track, you will find they overlap. For example, the *judgment*, *perfectionism*, and *all or nothing* tracks are interconnected, but singling them out will help those who don't fully identify as a perfectionist, for example, to see themselves in *judgment*. You can also have a hierarchy of tracks. I might identify with one stronger than I do with another. Maybe there is a connection with *comparison* and *fantasy*, but it could feel that *comparison* is the primary driver.

Be as *objective* as you can as you're looking at each one. Since the key to this process starts with awareness, if you find yourself rushing to defend or align with *why* you react or why you *should* be able to react the way you do, you might

> **We are all naturally aligned with our reactions or we wouldn't have them.**

not be ready to make the necessary shift to do this internal work. Instead, look at the track from an objective, observer's standpoint.

We are all naturally aligned with our reactions or we wouldn't have them. Now we can observe our reactions, using our logical brain. This takes a high degree of desire to make this shift. It's not for the faint of heart.

I have also included **Just For Fun** exercises for you to help build your awareness regarding each track. (Calling them "Just for fun" sets you up with the correct emotional mindset, right?)

Doing these exercises as you go will be more helpful while they are fresh in your mind.

Happy hunting.

Monster Track 1
Shame

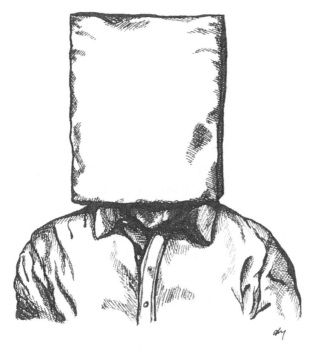

Truly, this is the epicenter of the original lie. It is the emotional nucleus creating the deepest feeling that *I'm not good enough, I'm not worthy, I'm not lovable,* and *I'm not acceptable.* This is the initial feeling that triggered Amy and created this entire process. *It's the granddaddy of all the tracks.*

Shame is a *flight* response. It lives in secrecy, because we can't let anyone know what's hiding under the bed, so to speak. Shame is the monster, even telling us to deny there is a monster at all, because admitting such could exclude us from our desired tribe. We could be shunned and cast off. Shame is the scariest of all the tracks.

Thinking back, my first memory of shame is when my grandfather had just died. I was eight years old and the youngest of 16 grandchildren. The only thing I remember about his funeral was riding in a car with some of my family. At that time, I did not understand the gravity of death, but I loved that our family was all together. It felt like a special occasion. Plus, we were all dressed up. I remember saying in a very relaxed, content tone, "What a nice day this is. I'm happy we're all here having this celebration."

I was quickly shut down by one of my cousins, who said, "This isn't a celebration, Kim. This is one of the worst days of our lives."

I was quickly filled with, what I know now as, shame. I felt:

- Embarrassed for not knowing what everyone else knew.
- Bad because I wasn't more sad, and maybe I was supposed to be.
- Confused because I didn't understand what I was supposed to be feeling.
- Scared because I wanted to hide from everyone after my "not okay-ness" was exposed.

I'm sure this wasn't my first feeling of shame, but it's the first one my conscious mind remembers. I felt such shame in that moment. There was no logic to it; but monsters don't wait for logic.

A common phrase during my childhood was "Shame on you" or "Shame, shame, everybody knows your name." I heard that all my life. In the old parental tape, I can still hear it. I would *never* say these things to my children or grandchildren, but these were phrases with which I was raised, based on the consciousness of the time.

At times I have noticed myself saying to my grandchildren, "Oh, you're such a good girl," or "good boy." Because of my new awareness, I catch myself. Is a "good" boy/girl opposed to a "bad" boy/girl? This value statement is still rooted in shame. I am continually working on changing my language around this issue.

Guilt vs. Shame

Shame is present as a monster track and can drive many of the other lies that the monster has told us to believe. Its energy is strong and difficult to escape. It is the deepest, most destructive, and lowest form of energy. It is not redemptive. It is vile and the epitome of the lie.

Guilt is a temporary reactive feeling when we perceive to have done something against our conscience.

Guilt is a temporary reactive feeling when we perceive to have done something against our conscience. Guilt arises when I've hurt someone, regardless of intention to do so. Guilt calls one's logical self to make amends. It encourages humility and can help develop future empathy.

While guilt **can** be an effective engine for change, if you justify the feeling and stay in guilt, you will miss the point of the lesson. Pain can lead to healthy healing if processed correctly; but if one continues to wallow in guilt, it can quickly turn to shame. **The line can be thin.** When I broke my elbow recently, the pain was intense. I had to keep moving and icing it, so it wouldn't freeze in place. This was painful, but I looked at that pain as representing healing. I *approached* the pain without fear, by focusing on the purpose of it; healing.

Recently, I made an off-the-cuff, snide-sounding remark to someone I love. I noticed right away that it wasn't settling with me. They didn't seem to mind, but as the evening wore on, I was being bothered more and more. The guilt was eating at me. I finally addressed it and said, "Hey, you know when I said ____? I apologize. That wasn't nice to say, and I didn't mean to sound so snarky. Please forgive me." They laughed it off, but I felt much better.

Until I made it right, I had unrest. Guilt was purposeful. Guilt led me to growth. Guilt contributed to my learning empathy.

Shame is different, as its pain is not redemptive. In fact, I've learned that shame is a main contributor to substance addictions and abuse. It is usually accompanied by anger (*fight* energy) and the need to numb the constant chatter regarding a person's worth.

The chatter pattern goes something like this: *I am bad at the core. I can't do anything right. I need to make sure nobody knows how bad or wrong I am. Because I'm already bad and wrong, it doesn't really matter how many bad or wrong things I do.* Sometimes the chatter can convince a person to become even worse: *I have no way out of this, so I might as well be REALLY bad!*

Shame is not benign. It stops us from being who we are truly meant to be and from having authentic relationships with people we love. We hold our true selves back for fear the world won't accept us as we are.

Brené Brown echoes, or rather sparks, this thought. Any discussion of shame cannot, in good conscience for me, leave her wisdom out. In her book *The Gifts of Imperfection*, Brown discusses the merits of casting off shame and acknowledging our own imperfections.

She writes, "Knowing ourselves matters, but not as much as loving ourselves. It's about the willingness to be imperfect; to be vulnerable. It's about the courage to wake up in the morning and acknowledge that no matter what gets done and what doesn't get done, that I'm *enough*, and that I'm worthy of love, belonging, and joy."

In that, she not only diffuses shame but cuts at the heart of the very lie the monster has told us. If one **authentically** connects with the truth that they are *enough*, none of the monster tracks will be present in their life and none of the incessant chatter will be believed.

Many successful business people have been driven to prove their worth by high earnings and rank advancement. Nick, a high-level, ethnic minority sales executive I worked with, was driven from the shame of his youth. He had felt *"less than"* so much during his life that he heard chatter relentlessly pushing him to accomplish and earn more, so he could produce and *prove* his worth to himself. He was tired and empty by the time we worked together. It didn't matter how much he earned or ladders he climbed, he never felt "enough". Shame's voice echoed in the depths of his psyche.

In my work as a health coach, I've seen shame wreak havoc on the minds of those who hate their bodies. Many people, especially women, have been raised with the incessant visual messages that in order for them to be of worth, their bodies need to look a certain way. As a result of the demand in the marketplace, media and magazine outlets know what sells, and they prey upon those who will buy their magazines, or the next gimmick diet.

One of my mentors in health and best-selling author of the book *The Habits of Health*, Dr. Wayne Scott Andersen, reiterated this truth over and over: "Diets don't work! Without changing your underlying habits to support long term health, you will not create sustainable change."

Here is an example of what I've seen from my experience:

Susie, a client of mine, was doing well with her eating plan. She originally was dieting, as it is with many, because she hated her body. Shame was her constant companion. Regardless, Susie was powering through, holding true to her diet – until she gave into temptation one night out with her friends. She ate something slightly off her strict eating program.

What she actually ate wasn't a big deal, but shame kicked in. So did chatter. *Yeah, that's like me. That's how*

I am. I never can stick to a diet. And chatter can get even worse and begin to bargain. It says, *You know what? You're already off, so go ahead and just eat everything tonight 'cause you can start again tomorrow. Or better yet, you might as well wait until next Monday. You better eat everything you can now. Monday will be here before you know it, and you know what that will mean:* **NO MORE GOOD FOOD FOR YOU FOR A LONG TIME!**

Shame and chatter drive their point home, and you indulge in that "Last Supper" night after night because you're going to start again tomorrow or Monday or after the holidays, and so on. You have *day one* after *day one*, or *week one* every Monday.

Shame keeps you stuck. Once this spoke is released, you will start to realize your inherent value. Once you *get clear on who you truly are*, you can start hearing your deepest, intrinsic desires for health.

Just for Fun

In complete privacy and safety, jot down a couple of things that you are hiding from everyone. What would be the worst thing people could think or know about you?

When we get it out of our heads, even just to write it down for ourselves to see, sometimes that is enough for us to release this spoke of the wheel.

If you want to take it another step further – find a trusted friend and tell them what you wrote down. Keep reading; I will give you some more ideas and tools to help with this as well.

Monster Track 2
People Pleasing

We all want people to like us. It's in our DNA to make sure that we are accepted in our social environment. Our young self had an internal radar to make sure we were accepted. As explained earlier in the book, we are constantly making and/or embedding decisions about ourselves. The constant question is being asked – *Do you like me? Am I okay? How about now?* From birth to three-years-old, we produce more than a million neural connections per second with the instinctual survival threat on alert. Even sleeping babies' cortisol levels increase if there are angry or upset voices around them.

One of the first monster strategies we were given was to make sure people in our environment were happy with us, so we would be accepted. Illogically and emotionally, the *fight* message was **MAKE THEM HAPPY AT ALL COSTS!** These emotions laid down strong mental wiring that led to behavior that, as adults, can easily continue.

The Parent Trap

This track starts in our earliest relationships. Our parents are the first people we seek to please. The genesis of this process, for many of us, dominates the rest of our lives. We are continually trapped in that four-year-old selves' mindset, thinking, *Am I okay? How do I make you happy? I need to make you happy.* As adults, it defies our logical sense. We can't figure out why we continue to **have** to make our parents happy.

This turns into a dance, of sorts, that we will engage in with many people in our lives. Our parents know how to push certain buttons. That's their dance step. Then we respond with our dance step. Even if it's an unhealthy dance, we're used to it. At 45 if you still feel the need to make your mom happy, proud, or not anger or disappoint her, you know this track is unhealthily affecting your life.

You might be saying, "What's wrong with making people happy?" And you are correct – nothing. But this is a track where you are stuck, and you know it. **It drives you.** Making people happy *at your expense* is where this track turns toxic.

Here is a list of qualities you may have if you are a people pleaser. Examine your reactions to the answers carefully.

You may be a people pleaser:

- If it's painful to say "No."
- If you feel compelled to not let people down.
- If you apologize continually, and you don't really know why.
- If the first words out of your mouth are "I'm sorry. I'm sorry."
- If you find yourself going into long justifications and explanations for things.
- If you avoid conflict at all costs. "Oh, no! We *cannot* have conflict!"

When I was young, and my parents divorced, I remember staying with my dad for just a couple of weeks every summer and sometimes at Christmas. To Little-Kimmy, my dad was my hero; my knight in shining armor. I **really** wanted him to love me.

One of the things I used to do was worry about money, thinking, "If I make him spend money on me, he might not like me." When we went to a restaurant, I ordered the cheapest thing on the menu and drank only water. I never had anything extra. I had to make sure I was as little of a nuisance as possible, even though he never said as much. In fact, he was always more than generous, but Little-Kimmy could not take any chances. She had to make sure he loved her!

These illogical feelings when we are young create these habits of thought and emotion. These habits follow us into adulthood. But again, we don't know why and where they come from.

One of my clients, Kate, was stuck in this same pattern. She told me one evening she had to go to dinner with her mom. Her tone was frustrated, so I inquired why.

She said, "Well, we're going out to dinner, but I have to go pick her up."

"Where does your mom live?" I asked.

"About an hour away. I'm just ..." She couldn't finish the sentence.

I could tell in her voice this was not something she wanted to do. She had limited time, and now she had to go completely out of her way, so she and her mom could spend a couple of hours together, and then take another hour to take her back. It was just too much. Kate works full-time and has only weekends off to do anything. Her mom was asking for a ride on a weekend night.

So, I asked, "Is your mom not capable of driving?"

"Yeah, she's capable of driving. She just doesn't want to."

"Well, does she know you don't want to?"

"No. I can't tell her that."

"Well, why not?"

"She just would rather me drive."

And then I asked, "Well, have you been honest with her about how you feel?"

"No, because it would just hurt her feelings."

This is the exact scenario that we've all played out:
1. We feel like we *have* to do something.
2. We **aren't honest** with people, because it would hurt them.
3. We are not happy, because we feel forced; so we become a victim.
4. Then **we** feel resentment toward the person we weren't honest with to begin with.

Maybe Kate's mom would be fine driving herself. Maybe she'd say, "Oh, honey, I didn't even think of that. You're right. Why don't we go somewhere else so if you do pick me up, you aren't going out of your way? Or maybe we can even meet halfway."

It's important to come up with **solutions**. Don't just remain in this dance; the tango where you **have** to do something you really don't want to do. Kate made this shift. She took the chance and risked this conversation with her mom.

Questioning Kate about this interaction, I asked, "When you had this conversation with your mom, were you upset at all? Did you bring it up in an angry or hurt way?"

She said, "No, I just said, 'Mom, I have such limited time, but I want to spend time with you. I'm finding that I spend too much of the time in just driving. What else can we do to still see each other but me not have to drive so much?'" Her words were very calm and matter-of-fact.

Her mom replied, "Oh, you're right, honey. I don't know why I didn't think about that." And they came up with a solution – all because Kate was honest.

Kate was making her own life difficult by not confronting this monster track pattern she had grown accustomed to. Kate continued in this track pattern assuming her mom's reaction would be negative, which would start the dance of Kate's feeling guilty for hurting her mom, thus proving Kate was *bad*. This all played out in a nanosecond, illogical but uninvestigated and even rationalized on many levels. This thought habit says conflict is to be avoided, so Kate avoided dealing with it, which kept the dysfunctional dance going endlessly.

Chatter tells us things like: *Leave it alone - You know what happened last time - Nothing will change - It's always been this way. What difference will it make?* This leads us to not address situations in a healthy way, and we keep our feelings and thoughts stuffed inside us. The ironic thing is, this builds resentment toward the person we aren't honest with, and the conflict gets bigger until then *WE BLOW UP!* We get upset with *them*, when **we** were the one who wasn't honest in the beginning. Relationships are harmed or destroyed all because we don't want the conflict. Under the guise of not wanting anyone to

Under the guise of not wanting anyone to be upset with us, and avoiding conflict, we get exactly what we don't want: More hurt and conflict!

be upset with us, and avoiding conflict, we get exactly what we don't want: More hurt and conflict!

Until we are willing to investigate (observe) and see the unhealthy pattern that our *people pleasing* track produces, chatter, and the bloodhounds working together, will convince us to make the other person happy at all costs. The consequences of *not* doing so can seem dire. The young child in us has already set us up for this habit, and until we see it for what it is, we will stay driven to make others happy at the expense of our own desires.

I'm not saying people won't be upset if you tell them no. In fact, Kate was fortunate. Her mother totally understood and could understand Kate's predicament, after it was explained to her. Many will not like you changing the dance step, or the status quo. You are messing them up, for sure! Changing the dance step involves some **stepping on toes**. You can expect some backlash initially, and possibly will lose relationships. Remember, they have their own monsters dancing. **Their** *monster mindset* will interpret *your* behavior towards them. Their monster could definitely not be happy with you!

A couple I worked with, Greg and Sherry, had a situation happen that has been extremely hurtful. Their son and his wife were newly married and living with the wife's parents. It was a hard situation, as the wife's parents ruled their lives with an iron fist.

Greg and Sherry wanted to help ease the suffering of their son and his new wife *so badly* they offered for them to come live with them instead. The thought came to Greg and Sherry to have an open, honest, discussion right from the beginning, regarding the amount of money and chores that would be expected of the young couple to contribute to the household, *but the parents were worried* that this conversation would send the message that the couple wasn't welcome. Greg and Sherry wanted to avoid anything uncomfortable for *fear* that, especially the new wife, would feel unwanted or offended in anyway.

The resulting two years were a **nightmare** for their family. Greg and Sherry were completely taken advantage of and also made out to be the bad guys. The newlyweds contributed nothing financially and didn't help with anything around the house. If either of the parents said anything, it inevitably ended ugly, with accusations being hurled.

By not following their initial thought and risking the early conflict, the emotions, resentments, and unspoken offenses were brewing and festering under the surface. The inevitable consequence was even more painful than if they had followed their hunch early on. Sherry said she would back down to "keep peace" but found her and her husband slowly turning into people they didn't recognize or even *like*. All at the hand of *people pleasing*.

You must trust this true principle for long-term health of yourself. We train people how to treat us. We can't control how other people will take it, how they will hear it, or how they will respond. You need to be (and can only be) responsible for communicating your *truth*. Be kind. Be loving. And be honest. This is really an honesty issue. If you won't be honest, you won't be healthy. And if you won't be healthy, the monster will drive.

People pleasers know firsthand the meaning of the phrase "No good deed goes unpunished." Either your monster-driven generous acts will be unappreciated, or you will set yourself up for a life without boundaries. In a life such as that, you will be taken advantage of.

My philosophy has shifted to "Only do what you want to do." At first blush, that statement raises the neck hairs. It's like *What? That's selfish, Kim. I can't do what I want to do. I've got to think about all of these people. I've got to put them first. I've got to make sure they're happy.*

If that is your response, truly ask yourself if that philosophy has worked for you in the past. Has this *people-pleasing track* created lasting happiness in your life overall? *Are you happy?* My guess is: NO! It's a double-edged sword. Your good intentions are just a monster track of proving your worth to people in your world; the behavior of a child looking for love.

Chatter will tell you to put them first. It will say, *"You're not as important. What will they think if you stop taking care of everything? Don't be selfish!"* And it will say this in your own voice and bring up situations where you didn't adhere to this philosophy and it backfired. Again, chatter knows your history – and probably knows it better than you do!

When you play out "Do only what you want to do," you will factor in the things in your life that are truly important. You will factor in your spouse, your children, your job. When you give yourself complete permission to not do something you don't want to do – a.k.a. say "No" - the world and others show up much healthier. Otherwise, we enable toxic relationships, and/or we live the life of a victim.

I had someone challenge this philosophy at a seminar I taught. She said, "I don't want to get up in the night when my child is sick. If I did what I wanted, I would stay in bed. You're saying that's what I should do?"

Great example! *Let's dissect this situation.* You are a mother. You are in bed sleeping. Your five-year-old comes in and wakes you up, crying, because he/she doesn't feel well. Play it out. What do you *want* to do, given these factors?

You can stay in bed. You can lay there and listen to them crying and throwing up in the bathroom. You can roll over and plug your ears, so you're not disturbed. But my guess is you *want* to get up and help them. So, my advice is: Only do what you want – and these factors will play into your decision.

I'm not saying we don't want to make

Under the guise of not wanting anyone to be upset with us, and avoiding conflict, we get exactly what we don't want: More hurt and conflict!

people happy. Your chatter might tell you that's what I'm saying. Personally, I love making people happy. It makes me *feel* good to do things for people that make them happy.

In fact, the sign of a healthy relationship is that I feel happy when I do something that makes someone else happy. In other words, I do it because I *want* to. Those of you who are driven to make sure *others* are happy and put them first, know the difference.

Another client gave me this argument: "I don't want to go to work, but I go. In fact, I hate my job."

I said to him, "Okay, quit. Don't go to work."

He said, "I have to."

I said, "No, you don't. No one is holding a gun to your head. Quit."

He said, "I have to pay my bills!"

I said, "No, you don't. Many people don't pay their bills. You won't go to jail. You can file bankruptcy. Quit your job."

He said, "I would lose my house, and I have two kids in college. I can't quit my job."

We went back and forth a few times until he saw that he was actually doing what he wanted to do, factoring in all life's commitments. He saw that he did want to go to work so he could provide the things that were important to him. He saw that he had options of staying with this particular job or not. When his perspective shifted to "I *want and choose* to work" instead of *having* to work, he shifted his energy and stopped being a victim of life and others.

Just for Fun

Make a quick list of those people or situations where you tend to be driven to say, "Yes." Ask yourself what you **really** want in those situations. Do you **want** to do it?

If you decide to say yes, *own that you want to do it.* Don't be a victim.

If you don't want to do it, lovingly and calmly practice saying, "No."

Another tool for you to practice is to tell people you have decided to wait 24 hours to make any commitments. Tell them it's a new strategy to help you not get overwhelmed by saying yes to too many things. Funny thing – it's amazing how many times the people asking you for help will find someone else if **you** don't say yes. Maybe we think we are more needed than we really are?

Monster Track 3
Judgment

This track specifically is full of RIGHT/WRONG, GOOD/BAD, and AGREE/DISAGREE judgments. I put the words in caps to show the toxic monster energy I'm conveying. These ALL CAP WORDS are strong, stubborn, and full of judgment.

From an early age, we learned to judge. We primarily learned this monster track by listening to our family. We learned what was RIGHT, and if anyone thought differently, they were WRONG. We learned to judge just like we learned to walk, talk, drink out of a cup, read, tie our shoes, and go in the potty. If we weren't RIGHT, the threat to our monster was too scary. Our positions, values, and opinions end up defining us. If this is questioned, our very souls feel at stake.

As children seeking approval and acceptance from our parents and family, the thought to even question these *facts* would never cross our minds. We grow up **knowing** the *truth*. There is a perceived safety in having a truth. The guardrails are up. We know the boundaries of what's acceptable and what is not. It gives us the *lanes to stay in* by having the specific rules laid out clearly, so we know if we've broken them.

Because the judgment track is so deeply ingrained in our society, we had very little chance of escaping. We did not have the logical, cognitive brain yet to question what was modeled to us. So, we adopted, mimicked, and followed suit. This is why children end up being the same political party, the same religion, and having the same beliefs as their parents (at least initially, anyway).

We were taught to be GOOD and not to be BAD (as discussed in the shame track). We watched and aligned with those who AGREED with us. And we ridiculed, argued with, or dismissed those who DISAGREED. They were WRONG and usually STUPID! And conversely, if we feel accused of being WRONG, our deepest identity is threatened, and therefore we must defend. We cannot be WRONG!

One day at a family gathering when I was young, I heard my Uncle Sonny say he hated Ronald Reagan. *Wait. What?! How could that be? I thought all of my family were Republican.* I had no idea who Ronald Reagan was or what a Republican was, but because of the conversations I heard around my dinner table, I **knew** the *truth*! And the *truth* was Republicans were RIGHT and

Democrats were WRONG. I even wondered if someone could go to heaven if they hated Ronald Reagan! I had no idea I had a family member, and one I loved as much as Uncle Sonny, who believed something so WRONG!

That brings me to the subject of politics, which is an area the monster relishes. We often feel it necessary to give our AGREE/DISAGREE judgments to things about which we have strong opinions – even when they're not being asked for. And we **judge** someone harshly who thinks differently than we do. That's why the monster claws come out and why backing down is an unacceptable option for some people. It is directly wired to their survival – and you can feel that energy emitting from your newsfeed on social media.

I enjoyed reading *Red, White & Latina: Our American Identity* by Emmy Award–winning television personality, TV judge Cristina Perez. I discovered she had the same impetus to write her book as I had in writing this one – the division in our country and how to heal relationship wounds. Here is an excerpt that stood out to me and that echoes my observations:

"Once we've picked a side, why stop and listen to the other point of view – when it's so much easier to swim in the calm, comforting waters of what we think we know?

We've stopped listening to anything we don't want to hear, anything that is in opposition to our own point of view, or anything that challenges us. We've decided to reject conflicting opinions, seeing them as a threat.

In order to protect this sense of mental security and moral superiority, we go to battle not only with anonymous strangers, but also with our friends, co-workers, even family members. There are no victors, only victims, fighting to be heard."

In any potentially heated conversation, people only give up or engage in the first place because:

A. they understand the difference, remove the ego, and know that no one is threatening their identity

OR

B. the other person's monster's claws beat them down into submission

OR

C. after eight-plus hours or pages of dialogue on Facebook – fighting other people's monsters feeling the need to defend their soul – nature calls and they actually have to get off Facebook to go pee!

The "toxic loops" happen in an evenly matched *monster battle*, where each person is equally committed to defending their positions. These "political debates," therefore, at their core, are more primal than anyone would like to admit. If you think about it, the "facts" part is done in about 30 seconds. "My position is X..." "Well, my position is Y."

Then, instead of "That's interesting, tell me more about how you came to that belief" *(observer)* It's "I am going to convert your Y to my X, or I will die trying! Attack!" People think they're debating facts, but they're in an all-out monster war that cannot be won.

I've had many judgers tell me, "But, Kim! If I don't tell them how I feel, they will think I AGREE with them!"

Do you hear the fear? Do you hear the threat of their identity? Do you hear the little-kid, it's-all-about-me wiring that is **still driving**?

A book I referenced earlier, *How to Win Friends and Influence People*, by Dale Carnegie, is a bestselling classic. To this day, the principles taught in Carnegie's book are life changing. His premise in the book is that everyone is RIGHT in their own mind. He even interviewed people on death row, and they were convinced they were RIGHT in their crime. They were all justified in their own minds. My son, Nathan, is a criminal defense attorney. I have attended a few of his trials. I see how everyone has a story. I see how everyone's perceptions are *RIGHT* – to themselves.

> **Without awareness, being RIGHT will be what drives all of us.**

Without awareness, being RIGHT will be what drives all of us. Therefore, do you see why we have such conflicts in our lives? We know we are RIGHT, and the people we want to influence know they are RIGHT! Have you ever tried to change someone from their *truth*? I have lost deep relationships over this issue. I didn't know there was a monster driving me in this for most of my life or how to stop it. I felt so **RIGHT in my RIGHT-NESS**. It is amazing how much of my mind used to be consumed in judgment. Everything and everyone was thought about, and dealt with, with an ALL CAPS label.

These labels were a safety net for me. I felt compelled to make sure everyone knew my opinion if given a chance. I wore my judgments with self-righteous pride. I felt noble, better than, and, of course, RIGHT and GOOD.

Religion is probably an area that brings on the judgment monster the most. Wars have been fought over God with the justification that because we are RIGHT, it's our duty to make sure everyone in the world knows, AGREES, and chooses our RIGHT as well. My personal favorite is *"It's only because I love them that I tell them the truth."* I don't doubt these people's sincerity in the least. But there is a healthy and helpful way to communicate our disagreements or opinions with those we love. When it has RIGHT energy driving it, it shows that the monster is using this chatter to justify itself.

(Side note: Haven't we all been taught to not discuss religion or politics in public? This is why.)

The Danger of KNOWING

"The greatest enemy of knowledge is not ignorance; it is the illusion of knowledge."
– Stephen Hawking

When we live in KNOWING, we end up being trapped in judgment. We are shut off to any "ah ha's" that would potentially be transformational for us. The biggest revelations happen when we can admit we don't know what we don't know. Living in curiosity and wonder is the path to self-awareness. Living in KNOWING is the enemy. Like the quote from Cristina's book earlier, "It's so much easier to swim in the calm, comforting waters of what we think we know."

Note to Parents:

This is a huge issue as our kids get older. As their hormones and cognitive thinking kicks in, this intersection can be dicey. If you've raised any teenagers, you know what I'm talking about. They need to feel free to explore what *they* believe. They can view the judgments of their upbringing as a threat to their individuality. The way this plays out varies from one adolescent to the next, but there are a few commonalities. They want to be free, and they believe *they* are RIGHT – so the same pattern of arguing doesn't work. It embeds them deeper into their viewpoint. Many parents, still acting under the judgment track of having to be RIGHT, and enforcing it, can lose their teenagers here.

My Suggestion: Do this work for yourself first.

As you become aware of this energy inside you, you can better navigate dealing with your children. Use some of the strategies I will give you later in the book or explore new ones that will come to you – if you remain open to them. You will be able to keep the doors of communication open with your

> child. Casting your judgment strong and sure – as well-intentioned as it may be – is the fastest way to, not only push your child into the situations you are most worried about, but also close off the chance of their ever talking to you about it.

Spouses already know what I'm talking about. After people have been married a while, their monster has learned how to trigger their spouse's monster. It can actually be a marriage of two monsters more than the marriage of two authentic people. *Trigger! Response trigger! Response! Wash, rinse, and repeat!*

This is not only directed outward. Many people report that they judge **themselves** harder than they judge anyone else. In fact, it's my assertion that *we judge others to the degree we judge ourselves.* Self-judgment is at the root. It's the constant stream of chatter that our monster inflicts upon us. And we didn't even realize it, until now.

Tool: Focus more on **how** and **where** you're listening *from* rather than on what is being said! Try this one on and see how it feels. You will become more aware of the judgment track driving than ever before. Observe how you are listening more than what is actually being said.

For example, when you see a post on social media regarding something you have a strong opinion about, you can:

1) *Align* with the chatter that *emphatically knows* your friend is WRONG and make sure they know your opinion in **no uncertain terms.** You need to "educate" them to the facts and the truth. What they

are saying is completely WRONG and ridiculous. After all, if you don't tell them, they may think you agree with them! You cannot keep scrolling without making sure they **know** how you feel!

OR

2) Listen and respond **from** a place of curiosity of why they think the way they do; not to prove them WRONG, but to possibly see things differently yourself. Rise above the specifics of the topic being discussed, to the observer's seat asking why they feel the way they do? This can lead to you finding the nuggets of truth that resonate with you. With this approach, you are showing that you are not attached to being RIGHT; that you are committed to **understanding**, not conflict.

OR

3) You keep on scrolling, fighting the tendency to give your opinion **at all**. You feel the grooves of the *former you*, with chatter telling you all of the reasons you should not let it go; but you take a deep breath and realize that they are RIGHT in their own minds. You send them a quick compassionate thought and congratulate yourself for making a new decision of reaction, one that can help rewire **your** deep monster- laid grooves, so as to create more peace in your world.

It's a process and it takes desire, awareness, and time. Many times, people are more committed to being RIGHT than to being happy. When the pain of staying in our judgment track is greater than the pain of change, we will do it. I know for me, the damage that this track left in its wake caused so much conflict and pain, I was willing to go through the pain of change. The results have been life changing. I still work on it, however, and notice the deep grooves that continue to pull me into them. I also see the new grooves that I'm laying, and I have hope that eventually it will be easier *not* to judge than it will be to judge. I have hope!

Just for Fun

Here's a little assignment for you, if you choose to accept it. Next time you are in a group conversation or in a public place, listen to how people talk. Notice in the chit chat the AGREE/DISAGREE, RIGHT/WRONG, and GOOD/BAD comments.

(Yes, I've been known to eavesdrop. People are just too dang interesting for me to **not** try to understand. Don't judge!)

Pay attention to your tendency to give your opinion, especially without being asked. Observe, without self-judgment, how quickly your mind moves to the all-caps labels above.

Practice the example in the chapter of how you respond to social media posts. Notice which response comes naturally to you. Whatever you end up doing isn't the point; the point is to *observe the mindset* you have that causes you to either comment or not. Don't judge yourself in whatever choice you make. Just notice.

Monster Track 4
Comparison -

"When you are content to be simply yourself and don't compare or compete, everybody will respect you."

– Lao Tzu

"Comparison is the death of joy."

– Mark Twain

Another sign of the monster is the need to compare ourselves to others. Most do this, automatically, without even realizing it. I know many people have this sick feeling scrolling through social media, where others are achieving, succeeding, and "bragging" about their vacations, their weight loss, their beautiful homes, cars, and kids. Even when one part of us is happy for someone's success, another part of us wonders what's **wrong** with us. We continually compare ourselves to all the successful people we see.

Chatter has us compare our weaknesses to others' strengths. It inundates us with the *flight* message of comparison: *They are so much better. I'm not as good as they are. I could never do that.* Or the *fight* message: *See. Look how well they are doing. You better get on the stick! You are lagging! Work harder!*

This track starts young. I remember when I was in PE in the third grade. The teacher would line everyone up and choose the most athletic or popular kids to be the two captains. The captains would then choose their teams. The most athletic kids were usually the most popular, at these ages. I can picture now, as an adult, what happened in the minds of myself and many of my classmates as we held our breath waiting to be a **chosen one.** God forbid you were left to the last! It was a constant state of comparison.

All through my school years, we all chanted "my school's better than your school" at every pep rally. We HAD to be better than *they* were, all in the name of "school spirit." Comparison and competition are highly effective for producing results, but can embed the lie deeper about a child's self-worth. I'm sure there are many positive things that can come from school sports, but I wonder how many adults today are a product of the negative messages they felt about themselves while participating in sports, with the constant comparisons and competition.

Think about your work environment. Are you constantly being pushed by your boss, who is comparing you to someone because they are doing better than you are? Keep in mind, your boss also has a monster driving them, and they probably don't even realize it. Regardless, with or without a boss doing this, we do it all on our own.

Comparison is an incredible motivator. The monster will tell us we are not good enough and can do better. Then the bloodhounds will use any and all data to somehow support that fact. We're never good *enough.*

The crazy thing is, on the occasion we find ourselves on top; the monster won't let us even **enjoy** what we've done. The *flight* or *freeze* message can sneak in sometimes and you become paralyzed with fear. People have coined this as the "Fear of Success"; it's really chatter telling you, "*You better not succeed, because you can't handle it, or you're not worthy of it, or you may fail.*" Or when you do succeed, chatter says, "*You got lucky; you've done it, but you only have one way to go from here, and that's **down**. You've managed to fool them for now, but they'll find out you're just a fraud.*"

Another area of struggle is the comparison of our physical bodies. Noticing the difference between you and the perfect specimens seen in magazines, movies, billboards, etc. can drive you to do whatever it takes to get your body to look like that. The habit of noticing perfect-bodied people keeps the bloodhounds bringing evidence of everyone who is so much better than you – maybe because they have six-pack abs or they don't have cellulite or stretch marks. They *must be* better than you and more desirable. The chatter keeps up a solid stream.

Self-judgment hits hard here, too. We beat ourselves up, we hate ourselves, and we go on yet another diet – all the while we are fueling the fire to keep the lie alive.

My mom taught me that there will always be people better off, and worse off, then I am. Her message was "Don't look at others. They have nothing to do with you." Regardless of where someone else is in life, their story is their own; their struggles and successes are their own; their monsters are their own. You can use equal amounts of examples showing that you are a hotshot or that you're a pile of crap; neither is true.

Over the years of being an entrepreneur, I have run the gamut of comparison. Do you look at the other businesses in your space and instantly feel compelled to BEAT them? The sales business, especially, is a mecca for the comparison track. I would go to the company conventions and watch the superstars being paraded on stage with the recognition, cars, diamonds, lights, music, and dazzle. Again, it made me feel sick to my stomach. Instead of (though sometimes along with) feeling happy for the person being recognized, I was all wrapped up in what this meant about *me.*

Comparison was a common issue among many of the people with whom I worked. Many of the people I coached struggled with this. There were many times that they'd complain about not being where they wanted to be or thought they should be. It didn't matter what level of compensation they received. I had six-figure-income earners tell me they were frustrated because they should be further along or earning more money. They would tell me that *other* leaders in their company were **obviously** doing it easier, faster, and better somehow – more chatter!

In a similar vein, I had $1,000/month, part-time, income earners tell me that they'd been working hard for years, and still they just couldn't understand why the new superstars were earning $10K/month so quickly. They aligned with the chatter that said something had to be WRONG with them! It was the same story no matter what their income was.

Their frustration had little to do with their reality. It was all based on **perceived** success of others, even when, in the big picture, they were accomplishing extraordinary feats! There can be no joy or fulfillment when there's a monster present. Fruitless comparison proves *you can never get enough of what you never needed to begin with.*

Just for Fun

Start being aware of this track inside you. Who do you compare yourself to? What area of your life does this show up in mostly?
- Your body?
- Your income?
- Your education?
- Your car?
- Your kids?
- Your religious service?

Make a note as you *observe* it in yourself.

It can be very eye-opening.

Monster Track 5
Perfectionism

An interesting facet of this common monster track is that many perfectionists wear the label like a badge of honor. They feel so noble in their quest because their *perfect* result is the golden chalice, the elusive Holy Grail. Perfectionists are frequently unaware that it's their monster all dressed up like something desirable, though, as you maybe already know, perfectionism is driven by the original lie.

The majority of people I've worked with who struggle with perfectionism, also had a parent who was a perfectionist. Amy did its job! To survive, these children had it wired that they **had** to be perfect to be *acceptable*. There are many areas where this track shows up. I'll give a few examples, but because this isn't a primary monster track for me, I turned to others for their typical *perfectionist* challenges. (Although, many people in musicals I've directed will attest to *my* perfectionism when they heard me say "*Run it again!*" at the end of a long and late rehearsal.)

> **Perfectionists are frequently unaware that it's their monster all dressed up like something desirable.**

A common area of perfectionism is in the appearance of our homes. If you want to have a party, you make sure your house is all together, everything matches, and the food is just right, because you need people to think you are as perfect as your home. While this causes great first impressions, keeping up the appearance of perfection is exhausting, and it's the source of many conflicts in relationships and families.

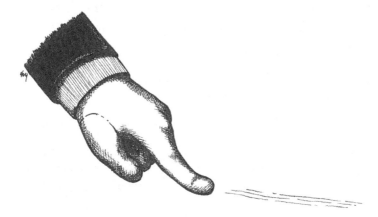

Is there anything wrong with having an orderly, neat, and attractive home (or body, or car, or refrigerator)? No, the issue isn't whether you have a desire to have things nice, orderly, and attractive; it's the drive to have to have it perfect, the at-all-costs energy, where it becomes illogical and toxic to yourself and others.

A client of mine, Stacy, whose mother was a perfectionist, told me a story of how she never learned how to clean or organize anything because her mother always did it for her. She recalled an experience where, as part of earning a Girl Scout badge, she had to do a household chore every day. She was excited to do this chore and to record it in her little journal. She was anticipating the feeling of accomplishment that she sensed would follow.

Stacy was eight years old and had decided that making her bed would be the daily chore. She had never made her bed before, as her mother had taken care of it *perfectly* all of her life. Stacy told this goal to her mother, who immediately looked anxious. She asked her mother to show her how to make her bed, and her mother proceeded to show her in great detail how to perfectly straighten the bottom sheet, tuck certain materials here, fluff pillows just so, and put the pillow shams and decorative pillows on *just the right way.*

The next day, Stacy endeavored to make her bed. She did her best – so she thought – but when she came home from school that day, she noticed that her bed looked different. It didn't have the imperfect-ness to it. She had told herself that morning that it wasn't as good as her mother did it; but she felt good about her job.

She asked her mother about it. Her mother quickly responded that she may have tweaked the bed a little; but she passed it off as just *helping* Stacy. Stacy recalled how let down she had felt and could recount many other things in her upbringing that her mother had just *helped her with*, which sent the message to Stacy that she *wasn't good enough* or capable.

Often, parents don't allow their children to "fail" as they learn. Their monster is triggered in making sure their children look a certain way because of the reflection it will have on them as parents. It is, again, **more**

about them and their perfection than the principle of training their children.

Perfectionists can also be obsessed with having their bodies look a certain way. The body-shaming culture in our world drives them to toxic, unhealthy behaviors; this can easily lead to eating disorders for some; others continue jumping from one diet to another. Working with people in health and weight loss, I met many of them. They were not going to rest until the last couple of pounds were gone or the little belly bulge disappeared. When the perfection obsession attaches itself to the body, we'll resort to all kinds of options attempting to match ourselves to the image we have in our *monster minds*. This is a dangerous mentality to maintain. It can end up killing us.

If a perfectionist wishes to be an author and write a book, they will spend years of research to back up what they already know just so no one can say, "You don't know what you're talking about." They might also labor over every word, comma, and period in each and every sentence, so the grammar police won't discredit their perfection – or think they are an idiot!

One of my clients was tormented because at one point in her life, she wanted to send thank-you cards but wouldn't dare because she was so afraid she would misspell a word or that her penmanship wasn't acceptable. It wasn't until after she turned 50 that she finally began writing thank-you cards, but only after writing them first on her computer, so she could use the spell-check. Then she carefully copied each and every word. In telling this story to me, she vacillated between bragging and crying. She knew on a deep level this didn't serve her. Again, our logical brains can often justify what our four-year-old selves' decided – if we are not aware.

A fairly common example of new enrollees in relationship marketing businesses are, I'll call them - "Molly and Polly." Both having begun at the same time and with the same information, their results are very different. Polly goes out with excitement and talks to everyone she knows about her product or business. She doesn't wait to know everything. Molly wants to learn and study the information in its entirety before she makes her first call – inevitably the call is never made. Molly will never have everything just perfect before she begins. She needs to read everything, start a new planner, organize her paper clips, paint her office, upgrade her cell phone, and get a new laptop before she can move forward.

Meanwhile, Polly, who doesn't even have an office or a laptop, and she is calling her friends on her commute home from work. She is excited and isn't afraid to tell her friends that she is just starting. If she doesn't know an answer to their question, she tells them so, and she promises to find out and get back to them. She's making calls before she starts dinner for her six kids, and again after bath and story time. Polly builds a **huge** business, and Molly keeps on "getting ready" so she doesn't make a mistake – until she **quits.**

People tend to buy the canvas, the paint, and the brushes only to move the supplies from room to room without ever painting a picture. They cannot begin, because they fear that the end result will not be *perfect*. Books never get published, songs never get written, and businesses never get off the ground, because perfectionists are afraid of failing, being exposed or criticized. Deciding to do nothing unless it's perfect is a definite sign of the monster driving. And in true monster style, nothing can ever be perfect enough. Does a perfectionist ever look at what they've accomplished and feel true satisfaction? My assertion is: **No.** There is always something more they could have done, one last edit or necessary tweak, or something is *not quite right*.

Believe it or not, all the research and prepping you do to create the perfect **thingamajig** doesn't work as well as good old-fashioned action. I recall a story about a pottery teacher who told half her class that they had the entire semester to create the perfect pot and that their final grade would be based on how perfect their pot turned out. To the other half, she told them they would be graded on the quantity of pots they created. She said nothing about how perfect the pots needed to be, just that the latter half would be graded on how many they produced.

At the end of the semester, it was no surprise who had the most perfect pots. The students who were simply going for quantity had the same time allotment as the ones working all semester to create one perfect pot. However, the skills and expertise that naturally came to them after making so many pots was more useful in making the most beautiful pot than was all the planning, researching, preparing, and perfecting of the other group.

If you are a perfectionist, you may have read this story and nodded your head in approval about getting in action without being perfect. Sounds good, right? Your monster, however, could care less about this study. *Knowing* this information alone won't impact a positive shift for you. We don't do what we *know* to do; we do what we are *motivated* to do. And motivation is driven by emotion.

The pain of keeping perfectionism going will need to be greater than the pain of letting it go and rewiring this track. I find pain to be the biggest motivator of all. If this is how you feel at the moment, and if you feel a pull that this monster track is hurting your life more than helping it, you are in the *perfect* place to make a shift.

Just for Fun

Practice imperfection. Be imperfect in something, on purpose.
- Don't straighten the picture on the wall.
- Don't fold your towels perfectly.
- Don't pick up something from your floor.
- Don't load your dishwasher perfectly.
- Don't measure something twice.

I bet you can think of several things you can do just from these examples! It will initially be hard to do; but let that feeling show you the power this monster track has over you.

Monster Track 6
Buttons

Do your buttons get pushed easily? Do you get angry at the drop of a hat? Do you regularly get offended or take things personally? Do you find yourself continually being picked on? Do you replay conversations over and over in your head and feel your blood start to boil all over again?

I have found there are two ways to not have your buttons pushed:

1) Inform everyone in your world how to...
- Behave
- Speak
- Gesture
- Drive

So as to NOT push your button -

OR

2) Lose your buttons!

Here's what happens:

When our amygdala (located in the brain's *emotional* center) is intensely triggered, our prefrontal cortex – (where our *logical* thoughts live) – shuts down. Think about the last time your button got pushed. Did you notice how the emotional part of yourself took over? Did you **say** or **do** things you normally would not have done or said? Did you say things you regretted later? The reason behind this is that you don't have access to your logical brain when the monster is intensely triggered.

There's a open wound, the lie, that is under the button. If there wasn't, it wouldn't create such a reaction when **touched**. If someone says something to me that was completely absurd, I would have a neutral response; but if anyone gets too close to the thing I am shamefully hiding from the world, the monster will erupt! The button is protecting it.

I've learned that button pushing generally shows up in two categories: (1) Innocent Attacks and (2) Deliberate Attacks.

Innocent Attacks

With these attacks, the button pusher never had an ill intent. The mental bloodhounds are at work here because when you're a hammer, the world's a nail – or in this case, when you're a nail, the world's a hammer. **Everyone seems out to get you.** You have a raw nerve and you perceive everything through the glasses of that original lie. You are a Ruth (from chapter 4).

When I investigate with the offending person, my experience proves that **100 percent** of the time these were perceived injuries. The button pusher didn't mean it; their intentions were never to hurt me. The *button push* was in a voice inflection; it was in an eye roll; it was in something I perceived as being there because I was **hypersensitive**.

Deliberate Attacks

Maybe somebody **is** upset with us or we are at odds with them. Maybe *their* buttons are pushed. Maybe their prefrontal cortex is shut down and they aren't using their best logic or reasoning. Their monster could be driving, and they say and do things they don't really mean.

Or perhaps there has been physical abuse by someone in your past, which can be described as deliberate. That can obviously create a deep wound. We can't leave it exposed and vulnerable – so a button is created. But we don't need that button when our wound is healed.

The Solution: Create a new interpretation. (I will go into more detail about this in chapter 6). The quick answer – not necessarily easy – is to employ our prefrontal cortex to tell ourselves a new story about the person who hurt us. We can acknowledge that **hurt people - hurt people.** They are dealing with their own internal battles. They have their own monster. It was never about me, specifically. It couldn't be, because they were so caught up in their *own pain*. It isn't fair, to be sure, but, if mindful, I can choose what meaning I give their actions.

> **Note:**
>
> I am not suggesting anyone overlook current abuse in *any way*. Having boundaries is extremely important. Being proactive in the behavior you expect from others is a healthy sign of self-love. I'm referring to forgiveness for those in the past who may have harmed you.

When I get my button pushed, I've learned to question my reaction. I started asking, *"Why did that bother me? Why did that make me want to punch him/her in the face?"*

The answer, for me, usually led back to a threat to my *specialness*. My go-to fear is the trigger that I am just average, a nobody – yikes! *I can't have that exposed for the world to see!* **How dare you, button pusher!**

Lose the Buttons, Baby

I was working with Ben, a typical type A businessman. We were discussing buttons. He said to me, "Kim, I think I have an anger problem. My fuse is so short, and I go off, it seems, at the drop of the hat! One of the worst things, lately, I've noticed are the people who drive slow in the fast lane," as his face turned to a deep shade of red. "They are complete idiots!"

I replied, "Wow. That's intense."

He exploded, "Doesn't it make you mad?"

"No, I can't say that it does. What is it about a slow driver in the fast lane that's bothers you? Tell me more about it from your perspective."

He continued to fume. "Don't they realize that there are cars trying to drive faster, and they are slowing down traffic, and that can be dangerous?! Cars will have to pass them on the right, and that could cause an accident! I mean, really, they are just morons!"

"So, how does being angry at them stop them from doing this?"

"It doesn't. I end up passing them on the right, usually honking and flipping them off."

I continued. "And how much thought do you think they gave it after you 'showed' them?"

He answered, "None."

"Yet here you are telling me about it, still all hot under the collar. Don't you find that interesting? You want *them* to suffer somehow, but *you* are the one who is suffering about it – then and now."

Here Ben displayed his button being pushed, triggering an emotional, internal outburst. He got angry, and yet on some level he knew that the issue was *his* struggle. When I mentioned this to Ben, he said, "Kim, that's easier said than done. I don't think I can control my temper in these situations. I have tried, but I find that it can completely ruin my day!"

I replied, "I'm not suggesting the person in the fast lane deserves your **kindness** or your **wrath**. *It has nothing to do with them.* I think you should consider how it impacts you and makes you feel."

The goal of living buttonless isn't for the button pusher - it's for you! You want to lose your buttons because of the peace it will bring *you*, not because other people deserve your wrath or grace.

Our buttons reveal the fear we have about *ourselves*. Ben's intense anger at "those idiots" shows his intense fear that *he* is an idiot. He can't have anyone thinking such a thing is true, so there is a lot of energy around anyone he perceives to be an idiot. His monster's lie was under his button the entire time.

When we feel our buttons being pushed, our initial reaction is to hurt the person who did the pushing. We are so busy feeling offended that we never stop to look at why certain words and actions hurt or offend us. The monster would not allow that. Chatter is busy telling us all the reasons that person is STUPID/WRONG/BAD. And we naturally *align* with the chatter. Remember; It's our default programming.

Note:

Don't mistake being annoyed with a button being pushed. There are many annoyances in life. They serve to help us learn patience. Slow drivers in the fast lane are that for me - annoying. Buttons are not annoyances. The intense reactions of having a button pushed feels much different. Watch the intensity of your reactions, and you will feel the difference too.

When the monster drives, the bloodhounds are on full alert. This will have us be hypersensitive. It's a no-win situation for us and the people with whom we're in relationships. We can even take offense where none was given. In fact, offense is always taken, whether it was intended or not. We can choose.

With the example of Ruth from chapter 4, she couldn't help but be offended that we were "laughing at her." Her *monster mindset* made it so she *had* to see it the way she did, and she *had* to be offended. *She was a button waiting to be pushed!* Her reaction reflected her deepest fear: people laughing at her. It became a self-fulfilling prophecy. My friends and I did end up laughing at her, so the outcome she feared came true. A great example of being RIGHT being more important than being happy!

Discrimination
(the deepest button)

I want to "go there" because I feel this topic needs some attention. We have perhaps become offense finders to the nth degree right now. I hesitated listing discrimination here in the button section because it may seem to minimize the seriousness of the issue.

Bigotry, prejudice, and discrimination are all in the same category to me. I see them as fear and ignorance based, a sure sign of the monster.

Fear is something that cannot be eradicated through legislation. We can't make people not be prejudiced. Of course, as a society we have laws that don't allow for prejudicial behaviors, and that is critical for initiating change; but laws don't change people's hearts. The answer to fear and ignorance is not more fear or force. It takes *understanding* and *education*. I could write volumes of books instructing people why they shouldn't be prejudiced, outlining the reasons why they shouldn't be, rebuking them for having such feelings, and so forth. I don't see the value in that, in this book. I would rather speak to the offended, the one who feels discriminated against, if you will allow me.

A good friend of mine, Jonathan, is a black man. He told me of an experience he had recently where he felt the sting of racism and prejudice. He was in an affluent Southern California neighborhood waiting to meet a friend, but the friend was a little late in arriving.

Jonathan was making calls while he was sitting in the car waiting. A neighbor had come home nearby and noticed Jonathan sitting in the car outside his home. This neighbor appeared nervous and seemed to be growing more concerned the longer Jonathan sat in his car. Jonathan decided to move his car around the cul-de-sac and continued his waiting across the street, still in view of the neighbor. The more Jonathan felt the negative energy of the neighbor, the more it worried him. The friend finally came, and both of them went inside the house to have their meeting.

About 15 minutes into their meeting, three white policemen knocked on the door. They had received a call from a *concerned neighbor*. They were following up on reports of house burglaries where Jonathan *somewhat* fit the description of the perpetrator.

After being asked to step outside and being questioned endlessly – about who he was, his reason for being there, his reason for sitting outside in the car for so long, and his whereabouts during the time of the other break-ins – the officers left him, and nothing more, externally, was done.

As a person of color, Jonathan had been familiar with the feelings of prejudice. He was feeling the biggest button being pushed of all. I'm not okay or acceptable the way I am, because of the pigment of my skin. *I don't belong here* (in this neighborhood) *with these people* (rich and white), *who view me as a threat and who have complete control over me and my future. I didn't do anything wrong, but my identity and safety are being violated just because I exist.*

Jonathan had done a lot of *monster work* over the past few years. He had worked harder on *himself* than anything else. He learned many helpful tools to help him cope with the dangers and fear he was feeling on many levels in this situation. He stayed breathing deeply and internally, reaffirming the truth of who he was, during the interaction. He kept his focus, as an observer, on his response, and not on what wrongs were being perpetrated on him, as best as he could.

He was angry and upset, understandably. After he left his friend's house, he had to pull over and release all of his negative emotions with a good cry. He could feel the emotions of shame, anger, blame – feelings of the old wiring. But he knew there was another response that would serve him and the world much better. He kept shifting his focus to his response; how he **chose** to feel about himself; how he **chose** to view these fear-based people whom he had no control over. He kept going back to his new decision, thereby embedding the new response wiring stronger.

He started a weekly video conference call inviting people of all races to participate in the discussion of these important issues. He used his energy in a constructive, positive way to affect change. He leads a large team of diverse people, to whom his example now permeates. He has **earned the right** to ask others to do the hard thing, because he has been through the fire himself. This is the kind of person who will continue the change of consciousness in our world.

Viktor Frankl in his book *Man's Search for Meaning* describes how he endured his experience during the Holocaust in a concentration camp. "Everything can be taken from a man but one thing: the last of the human freedoms – to choose one's attitude in any given set of circumstances, to choose one's own way."

Dr. Frankl's deepest identity was not only questioned but identified for annihilation. He was experiencing the worst discrimination and persecution possible. During this time, however, he discovered one of the truest principles we can learn: We choose our response. We can shift from fear to love.

Like Victor Frankl, Jonathan focused on his *response* to what was happening, focusing on **not** becoming a victim in his own mind. He refused to allow the fearful ignorance of the neighbor or the obvious prejudice of the officers to determine his identity. He had an initial reaction; but he kept moving to be the observer of this situation, noticing the former thought grooves pulling him to feel anger and rage. Because of the internal work he had done previously regarding his true self-worth, he did **not** stay in victim mentality.

When the discriminated are able to rise above the disgusting actions of others, things have a hope of improving for everyone. There are so many examples of how societies can change from the examples of a only a handful of higher-level-consciousness people. Think about Gandhi, Martin Luther King, Rosa Parks, Nelson Mandela, and countless others who have been an example of overcoming fear and prejudice. These people have **changed the world,** as a result.

I don't think there is anyone alive who hasn't felt unjustly treated. I know there are degrees of prejudice, and our chatter tells us that others don't understand our situation. That is true in all cases. None of us know the depths of another's pain. We can't control what happens to us, but with a strong desire for peace, and an increased awareness – regarding the monster tracks running within ourselves and others – we can better craft our responses. This will set us on a path few are willing to go.

None of us know the depths of another's pain.

As a result, we will see the fruit of this mindset permeate every part of our lives.

Just for Fun

Make a list of the areas where you tend to have your button pushed very quickly. My guess is that you've already been thinking of those areas during this section. In general, you might want to practice some of the responses below in advance of your button being pushed.

Internal Questions (after taking a deep breath):

• *What part of what happened or what was said got to me the most?*

• *Why does that upset me?*

• *What am I not wanting people to know or think about me?*

External Responses (maybe after another deep breath):

When someone says something that pushes your button unintentionally, you could respond with:

• "Interesting – you may be right."

OR

• "I hadn't thought about it that way. Let me think on it, and we can talk more about it later."

For when someone intentionally does something that pushes your button – or if you're not sure if the button pusher was intentional or unintentional – I will share some strategies in chapter 6 (Storytelling – Our Interpretations).

For Jonathan, simply taking a deep breath and continually adjusting his focus from **aligner** to **observer** of the situation, was what worked. Reacting emotionally in the moment is not a recipe for success – for anyone.

It will take a willingness to release this monster track, and you may not remember to respond this way initially. It might take a few times before you catch it. Nonetheless, the more you set your intention to let go of your buttons, *you will remember this tool*, use it, and find such a release of hurt and anger.

Monster Track 7
All or Nothing

This one is subtle. On the surface it may appear harmless. It could even feel like it's a positive philosophy on some level. I know I've said I am an *all or nothing* person, over the years, with a degree of pride.

How it shows up as a monster track, you will see, can wreak havoc in our lives. There's a lie hidden underneath this thinking. It becomes an either this way is true - OR - that way is true, scenario. It leaves no room for and/both. Without the possibility of a third option, it becomes polarizing. It's related to judgment in that way where things are RIGHT/WRONG. It assumes there can be **no** other possibilities – there are only two truths, and choosing one means sacrificing the other, and vice versa. While this might seem like decisiveness, the *all or nothing* track does not serve us. We use it as a **weapon** against ourselves in many ways. Because of the trap feature of it, we live in only one of *two* truths of (1) giving one's all or (2) giving nothing. Thus, it can be a cause of **burnout** and **hopelessness**. I've seen it show up within myself over the years in many areas.

My experience in the health and weight loss business showed the *all or nothing* mindset is rampant. When a dieter is **on**, then they are *all in*! They are on fire! Everything is good! But add any slight deviation to that strict plan, and the towel is thrown in. Then it is *nothing*, and one may just as well eat *everything* – because the diet is **off**. And those are the options many see: *all or nothing*.

This kind of trap is damaging to the psyche. It happens in my life with exercise. When I attempt to start a new exercise program, my chatter says, "*Well, you know you're never gonna do this regularly. You always start this, but you never finish. You never stay true. You're never consistent.*"

So many times, I have listened to that chatter, *aligned* with it, and never started. And my chatter justifies it using the *all or nothing* track. It says, "*If you can't really do it every day for an hour or two, and get your heart rate up, and work your muscles all the time, you will lose them.*"

And when I don't challenge that thought, I agree and do *nothing*, because I can't do *everything*.

It shows up in business as well. A sales client I worked with discussed how this showed up in her world. In talking about this mode of thinking, she said, "I'll get fired up, and I will work my tail off for four, five, six days straight. I'm just **ALL, ALL, ALL**! That's all I do. My family feels neglected because I work this hard. But I don't want to lose this momentum. I think I *have* to do it like this when I work.

By the end of that time period, I am burned out. I hate it. I hate my life. I hate my business. I hate myself. I have resentment, and I end up just crashing and **binge-watching** Netflix for a week, because I haven't fulfilled goals. I beat myself up for allowing my family to be neglected the week prior. I beat myself up because I'm such a loser and a slacker. And I continue this until I get fired up again to restart that whole cycle."

Our Relationships

All or nothing can apply to our relationships with others, as well. When we label people, it is difficult for them to ever show up differently – to us, anyway. This is because of the mental bloodhounds, and they are very thorough. The bloodhounds keep us in the *all or nothing* truth regarding others.

Once you have an *always* opinion about someone, it is difficult for that to be disproven. For example, if you perceive your teenage son is totally lazy, then chatter will tell you, *Oh my gosh. He never picks up his socks, never picks up his dishes. He always leaves things lying around.* That is all we will ever notice, and *they* can feel our judgment on a sub-verbal level.

This hearkens back to the Wayne Dyer quote from the mental bloodhound chapter. When you change the way you look at people, the people you look at will change. This is either because of existing evidence that is already there – but you aren't able to see because of your belief about them, (and the work of the bloodhounds) – and/or it's because they feel a new *truth* emitting from you toward **them**.

When you change the way you look at people, the people you look at will change.

Then, my personal favorite aspect of this monster track is how we can exaggerate situations in order to **justify** our *all or nothing* mindset. For example, a friend of mine, whose husband was notably frugal, told me about a time when she wanted to give some money to charity. When she suggested donating, this pushed her husband's button, and he responded in his *all or nothing* track, saying, "What are you thinking? Are we just going to **give** away *all* of our money?" He could not see there could be another option. An *and/both* option would be giving an appropriate amount, leaving plenty for paying their bills and saving to satisfy his financial desires.

Whenever I hear myself say the words always/never, I become suspicious of my own thought. In fact, I almost started this chapter with *all or nothing* is **always** a monster track!

Stephen Covey wrote a book called *The 3rd Alternative*, the message of which is: *There is your way, there is my way, and then there is the best way.* For Covey, there **is** an *and/both* option. The third alternative takes some compromise, but the result is peace.

When we question our *all or nothing* thinking to see the and/both option in situations, it opens up our brain to other possibilities. Ideas will show up. Options that might not arise without that first inquiry of "How can I see the *and/both* in this situation?" This shift can bring peace.

Politics and the Monster

The political climate in the world was the impetus for me to write this book, and this track is a main culprit of our world's division. When the judgment track is running, there is only room for an *all or nothing* mindset. As I stated earlier, I was raised a conservative Republican. The tenants of that philosophy that resonate with me, as an adult, are:

1) Take responsibility for your life.
2) Don't ask or expect the government to take care of you.

3) Tax breaks help the business owners, so they can pass the benefits to the workers.
4) Don't make it too hard for businesses to succeed, because that will impact the worker.
5) People take advantage of the welfare system and become lazy.
6) Enforce the immigration laws. Illegal immigrants can be a drain on our country's resources.

After growing up, when I took an **honest** and **open** look at what the liberal side feels, here's what I saw:

1) A belief that society has it in its best interest to help and take care of its community.
2) A desire to help those who are truly in need and have no other way to help themselves.
3) That greed of corporations has widened the gap in the haves and have-nots.
4) That money is used in our government to benefit businesses or the already wealthy.
5) There are some basic human rights in health care and education that government should provide so our country can compete and prosper in the global community.
6) We should figure out a way to keep the illegal immigrants that were raised in this country here – as well as tweak our immigration laws to lessen the red tape and expense to immigrate here to begin with.

I'm sure there are many other facets I'm not addressing, but when I look at these ideas, beliefs, and concerns, I have to say that most people I know agree with both sides to some degree. The fact is, if we were to all sit down and lose the *either/or* mentality - we can discover the *and/both* option. We'd be able to **hear** each other's concerns and come up with meaningful solutions. *"This"* has truth *and/both* *"That"* has truth.

The 2016 election of Donald Trump as President of the United States is a case in point. People have been so busy taking a side, digging deeper in their positions, and hurling accusations towards each other with a level of anger I've never experienced in my lifetime. Add the ability to "let loose" on social media, and I have wondered how many lives and relationships will be torn apart before it gets better.

I have to say that most people I know agree with both sides to some degree.

This is, largely, a result of the *all or nothing* track. I know many people who don't necessarily support Donald Trump or even the things he stands for, but felt he was the lesser of the "evil" choices offered at the time. (If you feel your button getting pushed right now, observe it, breathe deeply, and hang with me).

I see the more these people are attacked, the more they dig into defending their position. And, when buttons get pushed, the *fight* becomes the focus and not the real issues. Both sides feel **violated** to their core, and neither are listening to the other.

After the election, I thought things may calm down, but things have escalated further. I've had so many people reach out to me privately, telling me of the **hatred** towards them within their own families. Grandparents who have lost their grandchildren. Friends turning on each other. Employees afraid their boss would find out how they voted. I even had a college student tell me he literally feared for his safety if he wore a certain slogan on a hat or shirt. I had a dear friend completely unfriend me on Facebook because I didn't take a RIGHT/WRONG stand with her about a specific issue. In fact, I was proposing this "and/both" suggestion in my post about a certain issue. But it wasn't ok with her that I was trying to see both sides. If I didn't agree that her opinion was 100% the *only* truth - then she was not going to "speak to you again, while on this earth".

My mission is to raise the conversation from the "muck and mire" at the ground level and ask a new question. "How did Donald Trump become President?" What were the concerns and fears that caused such a large percentage of our fellow Americans to be willing, and even hopeful, to see such a disruption of our government?

How many people have sat down with someone on the "other side" to have a meaningful and honest conversation? *Not to argue* or prove their side RIGHT, but to truly **listen** to understand the other side. To find the *and/both* truths that are there.

My strongest feeling is that until at least a large percentage of us do this, the people who feel **shut down** and **shut up** will continue to dig in deeper and more government disruption will continue. It could lead to a new kind of civil war. It has already started, I'm afraid, but it can get worse.

I also see so much good that's coming from the current situation. Some people are becoming more **aware** and awake to issues that are important. People are becoming less apathetic. They are paying attention like never before. But in the passion, the monster will rule, if we're not mindful. There are *and/boths* everywhere *if* we are willing to look.

As you shift more toward the *and/both* mindset, you will start seeing things differently. New awarenesses will open up. Anger will shift to understanding. Even in disagreements, there can be communication and **intimacy**. Our world, starting with ourselves in our most important relationships, can start healing.

Just for Fun

Question the assumptions regarding yourself. Be aware of the *all or nothing* chatter of the monster. It can use your own voice to say:

- I never stick to anything.
- I always quit.
- I never have time.
- I'm always late.

- I can never lose weight.
- I always get sick
- I can never do anything right.

When these words or feelings show up, observe and investigate. Ask yourself, *Hmm. Is that true?* Apply this test to every instance you hear yourself thinking in terms of the *all or nothing* track. List the top subjects wherein you have the strongest opinions, and give yourself a test:

Am I willing to see the other side of this? Would I be willing to have a conversation with someone who has a direct opposite opinion and truly listen without the *all or nothing* track driving? Can I find an *and/both* option in our conversation? I truly hope so.

Monster Track 8
Compulsion

All of these monster tracks are habitual patterns of behavior, thought, and emotion inside of us. Compulsion describes the feeling behind **every** track. I'm listing it on its own, because there are specific reactions that can be identified when looked through the lens of the *feeling* of compulsion.

I had a client, Mary, who was a self-admitted hoarder; she could not throw anything away. Her house was bulging in every nook and cranny. Her refrigerator was packed full. She found herself saving:

- Every bit of leftover food - (*I will eat it later...*)
- Every and ALL family memorabilia - (*It was Grandma's, you know!*)
- Every piece of paper - (*I may need it!*)
- Every mismatched sock - (*The other sock may show up, and then I'll need this one!*)
- Every stained piece of clothing - (*It could be used as paint clothes when I paint again...*)
- Lint from the dryer - (*Don't you know they make great fire starters?!*)

Mary was so compelled to keep everything, and yet she knew it was illogical. She could feel her button getting pushed if anyone suggested she declutter. Because she was becoming more self-aware, she realized there was some unhealthy energy driving this. This compulsion was affecting many areas of her life, including her marriage, with even her children feeling embarrassed to bring their friends home to the mess. But she felt powerless to do anything about it.

Anything that has us compelled with this driving, out of control, energy, can be traced back to the original lie. The fear we felt around our survival connected somehow to behavior that shows up as compulsion. If left uninvestigated, it runs us on autopilot. It is behavior that, on one hand, we're used to because it's part of who we've always been. On the other hand, it doesn't make any logical sense and many times leads to conflicts in relationships, dysfunctions in our health, and even destructive **addictions.**

When we react with compulsion in our lives, it usually doesn't make sense to do what we are doing. All that matters is that we *must* do it and IN A CERTAIN WAY. It becomes the RIGHT thing to do.

If it is not done, or it is not done in that specific way, we get triggered – or it pushes our buttons. It's a feeling of being *on rails* about something. The compulsion track is strong and chatter tells us to do *it at all costs*, even though we might not understand why.

I have friends who are compulsive shoppers. They feel a driving force to shop. Maybe it's the fear of loss. One of my friends said to me, "I need to go look to see if there's something I can't live without." Another shopper friend of mine told me there could be a "great deal" they would miss out on – I refer to this as **FOMO** (fear of missing out). One of my wealthier clients admitted that she had been poor all of her life and now she finds herself addicted to shopping, AND she is driven to buy the most expensive items. (I think she said she had 30+ Coach bags!)

Note:

Because someone shows signs of a certain monster track, doesn't mean it stems from the same place internally. Someone who hoards, for example, might be doing it because they have it wired that they will "die" if they don't have enough stuff; it is their way of being safe. Someone else may have it wired that they need to take care of others and may potentially need all of these things to "save" their family. Don't ever assume to know anyone else's monster or assume theirs is just like yours.

For me (even putting this in writing feels pretty silly) it was a compulsion to wear makeup. For a long period of my life, I would never let anyone see me without makeup. My need to feel *special* was connected somehow to my appearance in this way. This compulsion was so strong that if I happened to be running late while leaving the house, I would put my makeup on while steering my car with my knee!

I would go crazy about my makeup, and anyone that got in my path would feel the wrath. I recognize now it was entirely an irrational reaction and a compulsion. Again, this stems back to the thought of me not being *special enough* and all this *fight* energy found in my old wiring.

Some other examples of some people's compulsions include:

- I MUST be on time!
- The sheets or towels MUST be folded and put away precisely *like this.*
- My bank account CANNOT get below ____.
- My weight CANNOT get above ____.
- I HAVE to get straight A's in school!
- I CANNOT leave food on my plate or my children's plates!
- I MUST be the first to buy the newest electronic gadget!
- I MUST work out every day.
- I MUST serve in my church, school, or community.
- I HAVE to bite my nails
- I MUST wash my hands constantly (so much so, they bleed)

There isn't anything inherently dysfunctional with having efficient systems, standards, or goals. Where it can turn damaging is if the energy about it is so intense that it negatively affects yourself or others in the doing of it.

The feeling is: *All is NOT RIGHT with the world UNLESS....*

It's another *at-all-costs* necessity. No matter who I hurt or who gets in the way.

I've seen people have compulsion over their coffee in the morning or their wine in the evening. Compulsion can also lead to addiction. While not all compulsions can be considered addictions, addictions are a form of compulsion. You know it's bad for you, but you can't seem to stop. All of these are monster driven. And the way compulsion is connected to addiction is a huge subject worthy of a book all on its own.

I feel a compulsion every time I hear a ding on my phone or see a notification. I feel like Pavlov's dogs. My phone has created a mental wiring inside me. It has been proven that we get a dopamine hit every time we hear a ding or get a "like" on social media. It speaks directly to our most inner need – to be loved. When we get that coveted notification, it confirms what we needed to disprove the lie. *I must be important. Look at how many people liked or commented on my post.*

My logical brain steps in to observe and question that chatter. It asks, *"Why do you respond to that thing? You're in the middle of dinner. You're at a family gathering. You're spending time with your kids or grandkids. You don't need to answer the ding. You don't even need to look at that ding. Let the ding go, Kim."*

The other side of compulsion is rebellion. In the past, if I had any perception that people were trying to control me, box me in, or make me do something, I felt a compulsion to rebel. I would rebel even if part of me wanted to do what they were asking!

You might have a little compulsion to rebel if your monster has perceived someone trying to control you. With responses to them, such as:

- Don't tell me how to cook.
- Don't tell me how to drive.
- Don't tell me how to clean my house.
- Don't tell me how to save money.
- Don't tell me to put my phone away.

It's so teenager-ish, I know, but I can still feel that rebellion inside of me now, at times. I'm sure I developed it as a survival technique, possibly from being the youngest of my siblings. Each of us was strong-willed, opinionated, and driven by our own unforeseen monster.

I remember a feeling I had as a health coach. If I ate anything unhealthy in public, I assumed people were watching me eat, and I automatically felt controlled by their *perceived* judgments. It created shame. I noticed the rebellious reactions I would have. Picture me, with monster rebellion, eating an entire box of Ritz Crackers in my pantry, with the door closed, speaking mentally to my perceived judgers, "Yeah! I'll show you - and the horse you rode in on!"

Now, when I feel a strong resistance or reaction to anything, I try to see it as my **monster alert**. If I can move to the observer's position quickly, I can look at my reactions and thoughts from a level above them – as if I'm **watching** myself instead of **being** myself. I can think, *Hmm, isn't that interesting how I am reacting to that?* From this place I can investigate it to see which part of my brain is driving. And, of course, it is most always the monster.

The reaction energy was my clue. If it's a feeling of something I just don't want to do, I have more **neutral** energy around it – like how you would feel if you had to take the garbage out on a cold day. It's not really what you want to do, but it must be done, so you buck up and do it. But if something sparks an explosive reaction, it is the signal to look at the root of the reaction rather than aligning in defense of it.

The compulsively rebellious Kim is still alive and well. Just because we have the awareness of these monster tracks doesn't mean we aren't continually affected by them. Recently, I was waiting to board a flight. I heard the boarding announcement. I became aware of a familiar resistance instantly present inside me. *I'm not getting in that*

> **But if something sparks an explosive reaction, it is the signal to look at the root of the reaction rather than aligning in defense of it.**

line. I can wait till everyone else is on. They won't leave without me. What's the rush to board?

Recognizing this rebellious energy, I had the thought to investigate. I followed the **spoke** to the center hub. *I don't want to be one of the herd. I will not be average. I am not one of the common people. I am so much better than that! I am special!*

Having this realization while standing at the boarding gate, I laughed out loud. Then, I got in line. I knew that old wiring was faulty.

Just for Fun

Make a list of those things that **must** be done a certain way or else life just doesn't work for you. With this list, be aware. Like the perfection track, do the opposite of what your compulsion tells you to do. You won't die, I promise.

Another thing is to ask those closest to you if you have a compulsion or a rebellion toward things they could point out. Sometimes we don't see things ourselves, but those we love can point to them right away. Make sure you give them an authentically safe space to be honest with you. Be prepared to hear whatever they say. Here's a clue: *Before asking, take a deep breath.*

Monster Track 9
Fantasy

The expression "The grass is always greener on the other side" serves as the epitome of this monster track. Fantasy is where our dissatisfaction leads us into thinking that *if* something external happens, **then** we will finally be happy. Basically, we will finally feel the love and acceptance we've been searching for all of our lives.

This track ran the show for me while I built my sales business. I envisioned the recognition I would receive when I was a superstar. I imagined how fulfilling it would be *if* I could be a top income earner or leader. Again, I was craving *specialness*! Soon after that, I achieved the top position. Achieving that goal didn't **scratch the itch** of my fantasy track at all; in fact, it just fueled it even further.

The danger of this track, is similar to a principle taught by Dave Blanchard, best-selling author, Founder and CEO of the Og Mandino Leadership Institute, and a good friend and mentor of mine.

He teaches "Fantasy is usually born out of a secret desire for ease and less stress. We use our gift of vivid visualization to escape into the future to a time *when* everything is wonderful and then play out vivid scenarios about *what* it will be like. We create expectations - concrete conditions for happiness. When life shows up differently, and it always does, we experience the antithesis. Cortisol surges designed to heal wounds and speed up metabolism; our amygdala, sends out an army of fear dendrites to shut off the energy rich parts of our brain starting with our prefrontal cortex; we are rendered emotionally paralyzed.

Let us use our powerful gift of visualization to receive inspired ideas, intuitive impressions, and creative solutions that ignite passion and drive action. Act on these impressions as if they were urgent assignments and you will experience *real* joy, not the counterfeit version called fantasy."

Like all the monster tracks, this one is an **illusion** that will leave damaging consequences in its path. It can lead to ruined health, torn-up families, internal stress, or conflicts in relationships and business, among others.

You might relate to this *if* your future happiness is dependent upon something particular happening – an if/*then* cycle. If you catch yourself saying any of these kinds of statements, it is cause for investigation:

- IF I had more money, THEN...
- IF I lose weight, THEN...
- IF my children were better, THEN...
- IF I graduate, THEN...
- IF I could own my own business, THEN...
- IF I was healthy, THEN...
- IF I weren't married to ____, THEN...

This list is endless. The key is to notice that your internal happiness is based on something external. This is a myth. Happiness is not achieved externally. You can't "get there from here." Happiness is a function of living in the moment; of shifting to gratitude, in spite of what you are wanting to change.

Often in the business world, especially when the numbers are going down, we will be tempted, by the fantasy track, to join programs, buy products, hire experts, and so forth, with hopeful desperation (fantasy) that *this* will solve *all* of my problems. When we look back, we can see that we had illogical expectations – based on fantasy thinking.

I've worked with many women in weight loss, some of whom will lose weight – and I think they look **great** – but they still see themselves as fat and ugly. There's just a little bit more that needs to come off, to tone up, and to get rid of. There was a woman who would repeat over and over to me, "*If* I could just lose these fifty horrid pounds, *then* I'd look good, love myself, and be happy." The **specific** number isn't significant. I've heard people repeat this with as little as two pounds keeping them from happiness.

Then never comes, or if it does, it somehow doesn't last or feel as good as anticipated. Many of these fantasy-riddled people keep going back on a diet, thinking, "*This time will be different!*" But in my lengthy experience, I have not found it true. No matter how good the diet or health plan is, if it is being driven by this chatter telling you that "*If* I could just _____, *then* I'll be happy," it will end in **disappointment**. Learn to investigate this voice. Chances are good it's coming from *under the bed.*

However, I have also known women who can shift to self-love and gratitude about themselves, even without perfect bodies. They don't have negative energy around their cellulite, their stretch marks, their poochy tummies, their saddlebags, or their saggy boobs. They love and appreciate how amazing their bodies are.

I've known people who love themselves **no matter what**. They learned to observe the negative chatter regarding their own worth. They started telling themselves a new story regarding their beauty. They learned some of the strategies (I'll share later) to stop aligning with the thoughts that drive this internal insanity. When they shift to pure gratitude, no matter what the mirror or scale says, they can hear an authentic voice of health that wants to be created inside them – as opposed to the fantasy chatter screaming in their ear.

An interesting thing happens when we make this shift: *We start feeling better about ourselves.* We start wanting to eat better, because we love ourselves and intrinsically want to be healthy. We start feeling the pull to exercise. A phrase I have used to help me get out of the diet cycle was *"I can eat as much as I want of anything I want. Now, what do I want?"* It's not driven by comparison, shame, perfectionism, etc. When my heart and mind feel gratitude, it helps me shift away from monster energy and into a healthier place, both mentally and physically.

Another example of fantasy can be found in academia, with the thought that getting a degree in something will prove that *if* they get to the top of their class, *then* they'll secure a lucrative career or beat out the other applicants, so they can secure whichever coveted **then** they think will make them happy and fulfilled.

My son, Steven, 24 at the time of this writing, has always been musically talented. He was awarded a full-tuition scholarship at Vanderbilt Blair School of Music in vocal performance. He received the highest audition score of anyone in the schools history, up to that point. So, you think he'd be happy, right? Oh no.

His lie incorporated the seemingly universal thought that he was *"never good enough."* The facts didn't matter. Instead, they triggered the monster even more. The **pressure** he was under (which was self-induced, as it usually is) kept him in a constant state of internal anxiety. To this day he works on having to relax and be happy; but he feels the *compulsion* to produce.

When Steven relaxes, he feels like he is wasting away his life. He must be productive, which is the *fight* response. Sometimes he has deep sadness because the chatter tells him, *I'm a pile of crap. I am worthless.* These negative thoughts are his *flight* response.

Steven is deep in this work and becoming more and more aware of his faulty primary wiring – and how to navigate it. He agreed to let me share this story of his development and then said, "But it still rears its ugly head. I often have the thought and feeling that I've missed my chance in life. It's over. My window is closed to any chance of success at all."

He said, "After that feeling of initial dread, I'm learning now to see this through new eyes, and I lovingly thank Little-Steven for his perspective. I still hear the echoes of chatter, but now I am much more mindful and aware where these messages come from, which helps me not align with them so quickly or for so long."

As he and I spoke, I could not help but think, *YAY! With the prefrontal cortex fully functioning **and** this information, he is now capable of fully taking responsibility of his life. Young Steven* would not be able to continue to wreak havoc in *adult Steven's* life.

If/Then definitely has a pull to married people. When we grow tired, frustrated, or unhappy with our current situation at home, the monster triggers the chatter. *If only my spouse _____, then I would be happy in my marriage.* The bloodhounds are now on **full** alert to point out all the reasons you are justified, showing you evidence of why you are RIGHT - and will also kick into full swing to **show** you the people in your world who, *if* you could be with **them**, *then* you would be happy. Your troubles would be over! This is a fantasy.

The reality of *If/Then* leads to misery in the end. People soon discover that many times the new brand of "greener grass" has weeds, holes, and thistles too. They just **traded** one brand for another. The promised happiness was not found; in fact, they **added** even more complications to their life, in the end.

Many budding business leaders have a fantasy of reaching a certain income or rank. They believe there is no happiness until they accomplish this. Though if they happen to achieve it, come *hell or high water*, they invariably still won't be satisfied. They can never make enough money. They can never get enough recognition. *If/Then* is never found, because (again, and again) *you can never get enough of what you never needed to begin with.*

In many commission businesses, vision boards are largely mentioned. This tool, in my experience, is a goal strategy that can trigger the fantasy track. Law of Attraction gurus advise putting all your material desires into a visual format, so you can look at it more often, dream about it, and feel the reality of it. It really ends up being a **getting** board, filled with the yacht, the house on the hill, exotic world travel, and the sexy sports car.

Visualization itself is a powerful tool, one that I've used successfully over the years in accomplishing my goals; monster driven or not. It is a law that *will work* and doesn't stop to ask or question *why* you have a strong desire for the things pictured. Your "emotion" is the command. If the underlying emotion is rooted in *If/ Then* thinking - that these material things will quiet the deep question of *Am I okay?* - **It won't.** It will be another notch on your disappointment belt towards despair and burnout, even while sitting in your Porsche or relaxing on your yacht.

Fantasy vs. Desire

A tool I discovered to deal with the fantasy track was to shift my focus on *being* rather than *having*. I started picturing who I would be and what I'd be doing when I provided the service that would impact the multitudes. I had material items on my vision boards, but when I visualized, I saw myself serving people.

I identify more as a speaker, so I started visualizing myself speaking to a group in my living room. I saw and **felt** them looking excited about what I was saying. I saw them come up to me afterward with tears in their eyes and thank me for what they had learned. I *felt* my soul expand knowing that I played a part in their growth and development. I relished the new friendships I was forging. Honestly, it was euphoric. I continued this practice, and as I did, I started increasing the size of the room, and as a result, my business, and the amount of people being impacted, grew and grew.

When your desires are based on serving and contributing to others, your financial desires will be taken care of - or you won't care about them anymore! Either way, you'll be happy. When you **need** these things to prove your worthiness or your importance, you will get proof of neither. You can't get *there* through fantasy. I know some people who smirk at me when I say this and respond, "Well, I'll test it out Kim, and I'll let you know when I get there if it made me happy or not," and **continue** being driven by the *fantasy track*.

From the book I mentioned earlier, *Man's Search for Meaning*, Viktor Frankl highlights this principle: "Don't aim at success. The more you aim at it and make it a target, the more you are going to miss it. For success, like happiness, **cannot** be pursued; it must *ensue*, and it only does so as the *unintended side effect* of one's personal dedication to a **cause** greater than oneself or as the by-product of one's surrender to a person other than oneself. Happiness must happen, and the same holds for success: you have to let it happen by **not** caring about it."

Pure desire, verses fantasy, grows when we start seeing ourselves with these new eyes. We start waking up to who we really are. We find ourselves reading, listening, and attending seminars. Desire grows stronger. It spurs us on to even more personal realizations, which continues to feed our desire.

> **Pure desire, verses fantasy, grows when we start seeing ourselves with these new eyes.**

Our appetite for meaningless things falls away as we feel a strong pull, almost insatiable, to keep learning and growing. When we are inspired from a true place – where our self-worth and identity are not at stake – we can then create incredible results. And these results are based on our **being** and not dependent on **having;** on us *giving* and not *taking;* on feeding our *spirits* instead of our *egos.*

For me, writing this book illustrates this process. For years, I felt something pulling me to write it. One of the messages my chatter told me was that it was just my being *special* again; that it was my ego. I let that stop me for a long time. I was tricked by chatter regarding my motive. Eventually, I examined the actual information with my newer brain.

I started **listening** to my pure desire rather than the warning of the illusory monster. This change of mind-set was and continues to be extremely purifying in the process. It helped me uncover the lie still echoing inside of me. By allowing myself to be vulnerable and as authentic as I know to be – and by continuing with the process that I'm describing in this book – my awareness of myself and the principles I'm expounding here have become even clearer.

When you look under the bed and find that nothing external will ever satisfy your fantasy monster, you can find your true desire based on service to others. *Internal peace* will follow.

Just for Fun

What if you decided to be happy now? With things *exactly* as they are in your life, now?

- Love your body - **as it is** - *no matter what!*
- Love your family – even if there is conflict.
- Be grateful for your financial situation – even if it's a mess.
- Start writing down *everything* you have to be grateful for. Some people do this every night before they go to bed.

Gratitude shifts thoughts; thoughts shift emotions; emotions dictate behavior; and behavior produces results, one way or the other.

If you use vision boards to visualize, **insert** the picture of yourself providing the **service** in your world that you feel the desire to provide. Create and live in the *feeling* of *becoming* who you would need to *be* in order to have the material things you desire, manifest in your world.

Monster Track 10
Blame

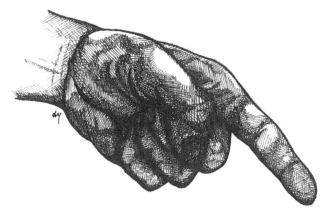

"Blame is for God and small children."

– Dustin Hoffman

Our brain automatically searches for a reason behind every event or trauma that happens to us. Blame becomes a *fight* mechanism for our survival. When you understand the early wiring of our psyche to be RIGHT combined with our brain's need for justification – all roads will lead to blame! Our problems, issues, and traumas simply *cannot be* our fault!

We can see this track **clearly** when we look at children. If you listen to small children playing together, you will hear it loud and clear. I remember this kind of situation happening during my childhood with my brother, Keith. While playing together, something got accidentally broken.

Keith said, "Mom, Kim broke the vase!"

I said, "Yeah, but it was **your fault!**"

Keith said, "No, it wasn't! You threw your arms up and hit the vase. So it's **your fault!**"

I said, "Yeah, but you were tickling me, and I told you to stop, and you didn't, so it's **your fault!**"

Keith said, "But you were annoying me by playing that stupid recorder, and that's the only way I could get you to stop, so it's **your fault.**"

And Keith said, and I said, and Keith said – on and on.

Listening to our parents, along with others in our world who have the blame track running, it's no wonder the thought process behind it is well underway early in our lives. And it only gets stronger with time. We **still** cast blame as adults. Not much has changed; we just use more **logic** in our arguments. The result is the same: *Whatever is wrong can't be my fault!*

Whatever is wrong can't be my fault!

I am a closet blamer. I've blamed everyone and everything my entire life. Combine this track with the judgment track, and not only am I not at fault, I need to be RIGHT about it! I am one powerfully toxic person when this happens. I have lots of damaged relationships lying on the side of the road to prove it.

Another place where blaming shows up is social injustices. Every time we see an injustice, we quickly go to blame. I mentioned some of this in the "button" section. Usually, this is evident in the political world. Whoever is the BAD guy or party, everything wrong that happens is *their* fault! Sad to say, but the following are actual quotes from real interactions I've had with people:

If it weren't for those bleeding-heart liberals, or those greedy Republican bastards, or freeloader Socialists,..." Fill in blank.

This book truly is for those who are tired of all the hate and conflict in the world. It's for those who are ready to be the change *they* want to see, who want to heal relationships – if for no other reason than to find their happy place again! We won't be happy if the blame track is present. It serves only to keep us **fighting** a war that will never be won; and it will destroy relationships everywhere.

So many adults I know blame their parents for their dysfunction. Our brains will always find a cause for all of our painful effects. Our parents (or ourselves, if we are parents) are the easiest and closest targets available to our brains. I've jokingly said, "A mother's place is in the wrong." Parents' monsters are usually doing the raising of their children. It would take the logical brain of children to **know** that parents do their best with what they have at the time.

I had my first-born at 19 years old (I was a toddler raising a baby!), and I was 34 when my last child was born. What a difference in my brain development alone; maybe this is why I feel inspired to understand the human condition so much. I feel a responsibility, especially to my two older boys, because they had a mom who was desperately trying to figure out her place in the world. I had both of them before my prefrontal cortex was fully functioning, and I was extremely monster driven.

Whatever harm is done to us is all part of the hand we are dealt. There are some who, on some level, have their identity entrenched in blaming their current situation on their parents, spouse, gender, government, children, job, education (or lack thereof), or upbringing. The mental bloodhounds make sure we **remember** all the reasons why we are messed up at the hand of others.

Until we are ready to take responsibility for our situation and realize we do have a choice, we will remain where we are. There are so many examples of people who, **because** of their misfortune, succeed. They use the "shit" of their life as fertilizer for their growth, instead of a sewer of blame.

Just for Fun

What are the situations of your life for which you tend to blame others?

Do you have issues from your childhood that you hold as the reason for your limits today?

Who is the person, or who are the people, you tend to blame the most in your life?

Make a non-judgmental list. Stay observant of your list, as opposed to justifying it.

Notice where the chatter tells you, *It's not your fault*; it's *theirs*. Pay attention to these areas especially.

Once your awareness is piqued, you will have a choice over your life – **blame and responsibility do not coexist.**

Chapter 6

Storytelling - Interpretations

"We don't see things as they are.
We see them as we are."

– Anaïs Nin

The biggest example of this principle in my life was my mother. She taught me the power of perspective through the story of Viola helping her in the kitchen. Though at the time I thought this story was for my growth, I realize now she was using it to rewire her own brain. She was creating a new interpretation for her life based on the happiness, peace, and joy she saw in loving, child-like Viola. She felt a need for change in her life so, she told herself a new story. She told herself Viola's story; "Everybody loves me and wants me around."

She modeled this to me all of my life. She felt that she could either worry about what people thought about her, and be always wondering, or she could just come from a new *truth* that she told herself: "Everybody loves me and wants me around." She told me, "I don't **know** for sure that everyone loves me and wants me around, but if I'm wrong, I'm still happy. The *Viola* mindset makes me happy no matter what, and that's **all** that matters to me."

After my mom and dad divorced I had no concept, at that time, what my mother was going through and what she was doing for her own survival. She raised three strong-willed children. She kept us in piano lessons that she couldn't afford. She kept us in church. She kept us playing, laughing, singing and traveling together.

> **A person's interpretation will decide their mindset, which dictates their behavior.**

And she was equally dedicated to her own learning. My mom went to school, either physically or by correspondence, most of my life. She had a four-year degree from North Central Bible College, in Minnesota. She became an LPN, RN, BSN, and, finally, she earned her MS in counseling, mostly while raising three *difficult* teenagers.

My mother showed me that a person's interpretation will decide their mindset, which dictates their behavior. She taught me that if I was unhappy with the results showing up in my life, I could trace it back to my interpretation, mindset and behavior. I could look at the results and ask, "Is this serving me? Do I like this? Is this something that I want to continue in my life?"

From this mindset, I am able to focus on a new story or interpretation according to my desires. This will give my bloodhounds a new **scent** on which to act, from which new evidences will show up. My new story will become my new *truth*.

My mom was also a master joke teller. She regularly told the story of a man who went to a psychiatrist. In the story, the psychiatrist showed the man some pictures. The first was a tree.

"What do you see?" the psychiatrist asked.

The man said, "Oh, I see sex."

Next the man was shown a picture of a car, and the doctor asked, "What do you see now?"

The man said, "Oh, I see sex."

The psychiatrist shook his head and turned over the next card with a picture of a boat. He showed this to the man. "And now?"

The man said, "Sex. I definitely see sex."

Then the psychiatrist said, "That's interesting. Every picture is different, yet you say they represent sex."

"It's not my fault. You're the one showing the dirty pictures," the man retorted.

That's the insidiousness of interpretation and how powerful it is. This man had no other truth as a possibility other than sex. "Everyone knows those pictures are talking about sex! DUH!" He couldn't see any other possibility.

Our autopilot interpretation proves we don't see things the way they *really* are; the truth is arbitrary and very subjective. Ten people could hear the exact same conversation, and then, during an interview later, everyone could say something different and swear their way is the *truth*. What they heard was through the filter of their own mind, beliefs, and biases. My defense attorney son, Nathan, has seen this played out in court many times. He is of the opinion, personally now, that unless someone has video evidence to show what **really** happened, *nothing* should be believed; even as truthful as the person thinks they are being. Eye witness accounts cannot be trusted, as far as he is concerned.

Our brain will automatically come up with a meaning; a cause for every effect. It is wired to make connections and find reasons for things, as I explained in the blame track. It will not rest until it has an answer for every question. It is a master "interpreter", but the story will be based on our monster, if left to its own devices.

It's no wonder there is so much conflict, so much angst, and so many problems in this world. Everybody is RIGHT, remember? We believe that our truth is THE truth. And because we see things the way *we* are, we can't see things the way they *really* are. Most people aren't even aware that this is how they are wired, so they live in constant conflict.

We Can Make Up a New Story

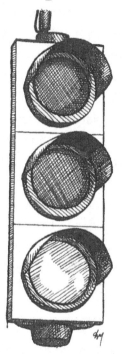

I remember in my early relationship marketing days, my mentor, Richard Brooke, taught me the principle of red-light and green-light thinking. In approaching people about our product or business, he said, "You will either have a red-light or a green-light interpretation."

Understanding both red and green-light mindsets are critical in understanding the difference between our embedded wiring. Once I became aware of these

193

different mindsets, I could see their presence and effect in my life. The red-light interpretation would say, "*They don't want what you have. They don't want to hear from you. You will bother them if you call. They will think you're selling them stuff. You will offend them.*"

This interpretation comes naturally and is complete chatter. It shows up quickly. When this was the story I told myself, I didn't make any calls, and no one heard about my amazing program. This resulted in **no one** benefitting from what it could offer them, and my business didn't grow. Richard pointed out that the red- light interpretation was a story I **made up**, and now I see why. We are naturally wired that way: We still fear we won't be accepted by people.

We have laid down those grooves of thought over time, so much so that we think they are true! Now, with the monster work I'm doing, I see why red-light is the interpretation that comes natural. We will always be worried about what people think of us, if left to the monster.

Richard reinforced the lesson my mother taught me:

- We can **choose** what interpretation serves us
- Interpretations govern behaviors
- Behaviors determine results.

*Morale of the story? If you want things to change - **YOU** need to change!*

I wanted to help more people and build my business, so I told myself:

(New interpretation) "*Everybody wants to hear from me - why wouldn't they? I'm their friend. They want to know* *what I'm excited about. They may need what I have. In fact, they probably prayed this morning for hope and help, my call could be an answer to their prayer.*

(New behavior) *I gotta pick up the phone. I need to let people know. So many people, so little time!".*

(New reality) *My business exploded!*

Is there truth in both interpretations? Yes. There's an and/both. Some people **won't** like that I contacted them; but that doesn't mean *everyone* won't like it.

There is also *truth* in the fact that there **are** people ready *right now*; and only by switching to the green-light interpretation will I have a chance of finding them.

I didn't know prior to making my phone calls whether someone would be offended, or if they were about to jump on board, thank me, kiss my face, and give me their firstborn. I had no idea how any specific person would react. So, I made up a new interpretation, or story, about it.

My new story *exhilarated* me! I created a new truth; one that served me and served the person ready for what I was offering. *Either story is made up.* When I understood this, my internal Ruth turned into Viola, just like my mom had demonstrated all those years.

Joe and I were on an airplane recently, and the flight attendant serving us was cold and borderline rude. Joe is always so friendly, so I could tell he was making some funny comments just to warm her up a bit. She was not taking the bait. She was determined to be cold, distant, and outwardly rude. As she walked away, we both looked at each other and started commenting on her rudeness. Right away, we both caught ourselves. (*Awareness*)

Joe said, "You know, maybe her boyfriend just broke up with her. Maybe she's a single mom who has to work and her child is sick. Maybe she just found out her husband is having an affair. We're just making it up, right?"

I wanted to **hug him to death** right then! YES!

For my businessman client, Ben, - who was angry at slow drivers – when he was having his "life in the fast lane" experience, chatter was inundating his thoughts with all the reasons why that person was a moron. *They're an idiot! They shouldn't be driving!* His interpretation was *how stupid those people were!* There is no room for any self-investigation in that state.

Once Ben could recognize this internal pattern regarding anger toward those drivers, he had a new awareness. After our discussion, it was almost as if he had **permission** to see it differently. He could stop and question his anger.

So, Ben **made up** a new story about those people. He told himself that the car in front of him was driving slow and not paying attention to the lane they were in because they just came from the hospital, where their child was very ill, or they just lost a parent or good friend. That story created an interpretation that led to **compassion** for the people in that slow-moving car. These new stories could be just as true as his thinking each of them were idiots.

Days later, Ben confided in me again, saying, "Kim, I want you to know that I was much calmer when

I drove today. I don't know what happened. I guess I just figured it wasn't worth getting that upset about it." (This is an example of *releasing a spoke*.)

I asked, "Did you have a fast-lane experience again?"

He said, "Yep! And I felt that same jab of anger, but then I remembered the new story, and I just calmly passed them on the right. I didn't flip them off or honk or anything."

"And how did that feel?"

"Pretty freeing, actually. I need to do this in more areas of my life."

How we react to others reflects how we feel about ourselves. When we jump to judge others, we show that we judge ourselves. When we have healed those internal wounds and rewired those neuro pathways, we will automatically exercise self-compassion, and subsequently find ourselves treating others with compassion, as well. We can't love others any more than we love ourselves.

How we react to others reflects how we feel about ourselves.

What happens when you must deal with a hard situation? Maybe there's an issue involving a family member, and you make up reasons why you *shouldn't* confront it. Chatter tells you, *"They will just get mad. It won't make any difference. Nothing will change."* Maybe you have evidence from the past to support this *truth*.

Have you ever wondered if the avoidance created more of a problem? Have you ever wondered if the expectation of angst created the ultimate angst?

When we worry what people will think, it's usually because we are putting our thoughts, fears, and angst into them. It's called **projection**. It's the crux of why we only see things as *we* are. It's so natural; we don't even know we are doing it. It's just like the guy seeing sex in all of the "dirty" pictures. He had no choice. He saw things as he was, not the *truth*. Without awareness and investigation, our assumptions and expectations are cemented in our relationships; and conflicts will ensue.

Joe and I once faced a monumental issue. In our 10th year of marriage, our relationship had deteriorated. We actually filed for divorce – and as far as I was concerned, we were done. At this point in life, Steven and Prosper – our last two children – had been born. They were young.

Joe and I found ourselves visiting lawyers, dividing up our lives, and trying to figure out where and how we would start over. We were both hurt and had hurt each other terribly. The bloodhounds were working overtime showing us why our marriage should be over. Both of us had strong evidence *proving* that the best thing to do was divorce.

Luckily, there was just enough desire to look at it differently, with new eyes. We had one last shot of changing the way we looked at things so that the things that we looked could change. It was hard. There was *truth* in our hurts and real suffering we had experienced; but we needed to tell new stories about each other. It took some work, as the *truths* of our old story kept sucking us back in, as the chatter did its darnedest to talk us out of our new story. But we persisted!

We decided on a new way of looking at each other. We started noticing and thereby collecting evidence that served our new story. We needed to **keep** making a new decision. At the time of this writing, we have now been married for 31 years; and I can tell you, we are the happiest, the most united, and the most fulfilled that we have ever been. I'm so thankful that we learned the lesson of telling a new story, making up a new interpretation, and looking at things with new mindsets. Things showed up differently, as evidenced by our new reality.

Changing our interpretations or stories about others is vital but telling a new story about ourselves is even more important. We will only see the evidence of what we believe. The bloodhounds will only let that data in. But when we tell a new story about ourselves *to* ourselves, with *accompanying **positive emotion***, the bloodhounds will have a new scent to pick up. They will start showing us what was there all along, we just could not see it.

And remember: *How* we approach a change is critical. Instead of cowering in fear, feeling powerless or hopeless, rewrite your own story from a completely new place. Much like my mother-in-law with the computer, pre-decide that it will be *ok,* an adventure, even *easy.* Take what you feel as stress, fear, or anxiety, and shift to a new interpretation; call it exhilaration, excitement, wonder, creativity, and it will all show up differently. I love the expression, "It's all good."

When Joe and I looked at our dysfunctional marriage with the thought *"This is going to be interesting to see how we can put this together. Let's see if we can,"* instead of *"It's over. There's no hope. We can't do anything about this,"* it opened up many possibilities. *Our new interpretation **saved** our marriage.*

A light-hearted example, in conclusion:

There was once a bright-eyed girl who woke up on Christmas morning. She ran down to the tree, full of excitement for the promised presents, and found a big pile of manure. Instead of being disheartened, she immediately began shoveling that manure. When her parents came downstairs, they found her working hard, and they were so surprised.

They asked her, "Honey, what are you doing?"

She revealed her interpretation shift. "Well, with all this poop, there's got to be a pony in here somewhere."

Each of you **can** tell a new story, look at things differently and decide on one that will better serve yourself and the rest of the world. Move to the observer of your thoughts, instead of the aligner and judger. Watch and listen to the thoughts running in the background of your mind. Better yet, watch your actions, **without judgment**. This will **show** you your interpretation and reveal the current story you are telling yourself.

This is the genesis of mindfulness. You can even start making a journal of thoughts - whatever they are. No judgement. No RIGHT/WRONG - GOOD/BAD. Just what is. One of the first books that made a big impact for me, on the subject of mindfulness, was a book, *Wherever You Go, There You Are,* by Jon Kabat Zinn. Until we uncover the toxic interpretations that can easily run in the background, we won't experience the pure joy that can be right in front of us. We won't be able to see it.

Chapter 7

Facing the Monster ˗

Congratulations! You've officially reached the part of the book where the rubber meets the road! Now that we understand how the monster shows up, our logical brains can understand the difference between what we want and what the monster is telling us through fear and chatter.

Run to the Roar

We can now make sense of these illogical emotions. We can decide to actually take a good look, lift up the bedspread, and say, "I'm going to look right into that scary place where my little self is still hiding." It's there we face the lie.

It will involve fear. The fear that created the lie still lives *there*; in your emotional pathway. You've been aligning with, avoiding, hiding and denying this fear all of your life. Now, with your new and improved adult brain, and armed with this information, you can *run to the roar,* so to speak. This starts with a decision to act. When we act, we send the message to ourselves that we are serious. We stop thinking. Where does fear live? In our thoughts. The more we **stop thinking** and **start doing**, the more we won't get snagged by chatter or by the *freeze* response.

> When we act, we send the message to ourselves that we are serious.

I have enjoyed the book *The 5 Second Rule* by Mel Robbins. She says, "The moment you have an instinct to act on a goal you must count 5-4-3-2-1 and physically move or your brain will stop you."

How does the brain stop you? Chatter – why does it stop you? Because you are apprehensive, stressed, worried, nervous, rebellious etc. You can expect chatter to that same extent. *It will follow the emotion that you bring to it.*

I'll share further, in the next chapter, how to rewire the thoughts that have kept us stuck.

My first *running to the roar* experience was back in the early days of my personal development. I was in my late 20s, and it was when I was involved with my first relationship marketing company. I was working with Richard Brooke in a leadership development program. It was scary and exhilarating at the same time. I was a sponge for growth.

One of my projects was to identify something that had a particularly strong hold on me. This was when I identified the need to be *special*. I asked myself in honest introspection, *"What is something that would be extremely hard for me to face or deal with that is connected to my need to be special?"*

In a nanosecond, my deep-seated need for makeup came to mind. Just the thought of being seen without makeup on, left me feeling nauseated.

I knew right then what I needed/wanted to do. I knew that if something like this was in control of me, I would not be able to grow or develop meaningful relationships. I had to *run to this roar*. Honestly, it had nothing to do with the makeup itself but what the makeup represented at that time to me.

I was about to speak at a company leadership event where my *special* distinction was sure to get attention! This was a perfect time to test what I was made of; to run to my *special* roar.

The morning of the event, I put my business suit on but purposefully left off **any** makeup. As I joined the crowd around the lobby of the hotel, it felt like I was standing in front of everyone - completely **naked**. I was sick to my stomach. I remember constantly reminding myself where the bathrooms were. I was shaky. I was sweaty. Chatter was loud. My monster was in full swing. And Amy was trying to save me from the impending death. (Remember, this is felt emotionally. Explaining it logically sounds ridiculous, right?)

Chatter told me that people would see me as *average* and decidedly not *special*. It screamed at me, *"What are you doing? You're going to be so ugly. People will laugh at you. You know ____ will be there, and she is so beautiful. People will know that she is really better than you are. You need to maintain your image, Kim."* On and on, the chatter **pounded** in my head.

I approached a group of familiar faces as I got off the elevator. I was on high alert for the smirks and/or shocked expressions. I was anticipating the **shame** that was sure to come. As you have probably guessed, it didn't come. I saw a mixture in those first 30 minutes, while mingling in the lobby, of love, friendship, questioning looks of "Did you do something different with your hair?" and a benign "Kim, you look so good au naturel."

There was an encounter with Richard himself that shook me when he did a double take from the stage and started chuckling. That sent me reeling, but again, it took some re-interpretation of that interaction, and I was good to go. I did not die.

People still loved me. People still saw me as a leader, and those who heard what this experience was like for me used this example in their own lives to *run to their roars*. My fears were relieved. My anxiety abated. Amy followed suit and calmed down, too. It follows our lead.

It was exactly like lifting up the bedspread and seeing that nothing was there. By the end of the day, I had started to rewire a dysfunctional piece of my psyche. And now I can act from desire rather than from fear.

I still wear makeup, but I do not **have** to wear it to affirm my value; I am perfectly fine if people see me without makeup.

This strategy works with any of the monster tracks. It might be something directly connected to your lie, as mine was, or it could be something as simple as procrastination. No matter the case, once you get into action and face your fears, you will respond by asking yourself, *"Why didn't I do that sooner?"*

Sneak Up on the Roar

There are variations of *running to the roar*, too. One is to *sneak up on the roar*. To do this, I give myself full permission to **not** do it at all or to just do a little bit. (Remember - I get rebellious!)

My niece, Bryndis, has learned the "sneaking up" process. She doesn't *make* herself do something she has intense resistance to. For example, her yoga practice. She was telling me she just focuses on merely getting her yoga clothes on. Then she will see what happens. She inches her way forward, getting her mat out, sitting down calmly, and still giving herself permission to not do it if she doesn't want to. And then she turns on her preferred yoga program. She gently begins the practice, and she tells herself, *"As long as I'm here, I may as well just do it."*

This strategy doesn't seem to trigger the monster. If the idea of exercise in general came to me, as I've said earlier, chatter would begin immediately. So, I learned to *sneak up on the roar* too. I would begin with *I'll just put my tennis shoes on. That's it. And maybe I'll exercise; maybe I won't. Maybe I'll go for a walk; maybe I won't.* Then I put on my shoes. *I'm just going to go walk to the mailbox. That's it.* Then I start walking only to the mailbox. Then I say, *Well, I'll just go to the corner.* I follow this pattern and have many times found myself going on a 3 - 5 mile run/walk. This approach keeps me **calm**. And when I'm calm, Amy is happy, the monster is not triggered, and rebellion isn't sparked. I've used this strategy to do many projects that I, initially, have a strong resistance to. It works!

A great reason to *sneak up on the roar* is that it gently lays down new emotional pathways. At the end of it all, you will think, *Oh, that felt so good. I love that. Why did I fight it? Why didn't I just do it?* (Without self-judgement!) Creating **positive** emotions helps rewire those old, pesky, negative ones. In the future, you will shift to an emotion of **love to**, **choose to**, and **want to** with what you were, previously, resisting. This is a much more **fun** and, therefore, **sustainable**, approach.

Resting to the Roar

Speedboats drive fast; their purpose is high velocity. Within the context of this book, speedboats are monster driven. There can be fun times, but when you crash, you crash hard. You **burn** up. It takes a lot of unsustainable energy to maintain a speedboat.

My friend, Bryan Franklin, CEO and founder of Outbound Works, was a life coach and business mentor of mine a few years ago. He taught me this principle. On the opposite side of the speedboat in this analogy is a sailboat. Sailboats are fueled by wind. In this metaphor, wind is the deep sense of truth, the real truth inside us, or pure love. Love is inexhaustible, sustainable, and never-ending. When we are in the sailboat, we can still reach our destination. In fact, we, at times, may arrive faster with the sailboat, but definitely with more joy.

When you shift from speedboat energy to sailboat energy, it's uncomfortable. We're used to the driving energy of the speedboat. We're used to driving our success. There's an adrenaline **high** connected to it as well. Personally, I often wondered if I was addicted to adrenaline, because of how often I was using it to accomplish goals. In contrast, the sailboat is an energy source of inexhaustible love and creation. There's no race, no need to *prove* anything. There's no compulsion track driving.

Sailboat energy will provide the intended feeling of peace, happiness, and joy. I can still work hard and fast, but the energy is not to prove anything regarding my worth or value. Rather, all that energy is directed to the goal.

In terms of *resting to the roar*, we can create new brain wiring. Shifting to the sailboat, for me, was hard. It was **foreign**. It was scary. Chatter told me, *I won't have winning energy at all.* I would not be able to be *special*; the world would know I was a loser, a slacker, just *average!*

The shift started with a desire for growth. It took seeing the unhealthy outcomes of my monster (speedboat). It took being ready to make a change because of the **pain** I was experiencing in my current monster-driven state. It took courage to lift up the bedspread and brave the risk. *Resting to the roar* was a form of *running to the roar,* in that it scared me to **death**! I felt lost in the unfamiliar world of rest. So, I needed to *face* rest, no matter how *freaked out* it made me feel.

My successful business client, Melanie, who feared defanging her monster because her business drive would be gone, discovered that the pounding energy to achieve **at all costs** had cost her many relationships, her health and had given her a deep sense of dread. She had little to no joy. She decided to give this idea a try.

We worked on it together. The deep grooves of the familiar monster were triggered often, but with growing awareness and support, she was able to make the shift to the sailboat. She is still using the skills, talents, and connections she always has, but the energy source has shifted. With this shift, she can truly balance her life. She can let go and not feel the weight of the world on her shoulders. She can enjoy the success she has built. It is a process, but this is what makes this work worthwhile for me.

My client Mary, from the compulsion track story– who saved everything – discovered her lie when she rested. She knew her fear of throwing anything away was rooted in something scary. She knew there were toxic elements involved but decided to stay in a calm, self-loving place. We worked together on this and she became more and more aware of this track, as it showed up. As she shifted her energy source, she saw her lie.

She saw how her compulsion to **save** everything, came from her being adopted when she was born. She knew that she had been adopted most of her childhood. Little-Mary had it wired that she had been thrown away. Every time she was trying to throw things away in her life, her lie was triggered – *I am garbage*. **She** had been thrown away. In a sense, she was trying to save *herself*. She was in *fight* mode which resulted in her belief that everything should be saved.

She had no idea that this was how she was wired; but she knew something was lurking "under the covers." She was tired of the pain and internal conflict she was experiencing. She decided to *rest to the roar*, and found huge relief. Was it still hard to throw things away? Yes. But now with her logical brain, she could make a new decision. She could tell herself a new story.

Whatever course you take – *running, sneaking,* or *resting* – the important step is actually ***doing it***. The act of moving toward whatever thing you are scared of will eventually allow you to grow. It's a message to your younger self that the real **you** will not be bullied anymore; you will now use the full mental armory at your disposal to face the monster who has been wreaking havoc in your soul, and by so doing see there was really only dust bunnies and dirty socks.

Chapter 8

Rewiring

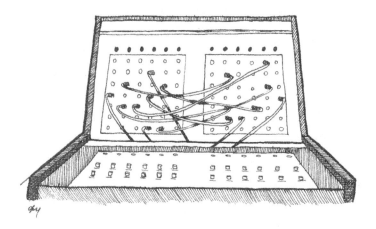

Sometimes people ask me, "What is the point of what you're doing with the monster, Kim? I get that I've had a lie at the core of my soul. I see your metaphor. I even see some tracks exhibited in my life. But now what?"

The answer is in understanding how our brain wiring was created to begin with. The Hebb's Law that I mentioned earlier, "What fires together, wires together" applies to the rewiring process, as well.

My assertion is emotions create the firing and repetition of those emotions create the wiring. Here is my elementary explanation: There are billions of bits of information being transmitted in our neuropathways per second. When you get emotional about something, these wires say to each other, "Hey! Obviously, this is important. Let's form a bond right here, right now. Ready? Connect!" The neuro pathways fire together. If this happened just once or twice there would be a *slight* "wiring" of these neurons. It could easily be unwired if the thought/emotion cycle doesn't repeat. (The law of "What we don't use, we lose", applies to our brains, as well.)

But with the RAS in the mix, the bloodhounds will continue to bring the evidence of why we are bad, worthless, unacceptable, in turn, producing the familiar fear that fires the emotional response again and again. It's wash, rinse, repeat.

We are the product of what our emotions decide we are.

We are the product of what our emotions decide we are. I stated this at one of my seminars and a man in the audience got his button pushed. He vehemently argued this *wasn't* true for him. He protested that he was driven *only* by logic and reasoning. He said he couldn't **stand** it when people were driven by emotions and that he typically avoids people who are like that. I challenged him a little on it, to which he got red in the face and exclaimed emphatically "I AM NOT EMOTIONAL!"

Have you been somewhere, and a song starts to play that you remember from a highly emotional time of your life? How many times do you remember exactly where you were, who you were with, or what you were doing? Not long ago, while I was driving, I heard Olivia Newton-John's song "Hopelessly Devoted to You."

As soon as it started playing on my Sirius '70s on 7 channel, my mind immediately went to 1978 and the **memory** of my driving to see my dad, who lived a couple hours away at the time. I was heartbroken because I had just been left by someone who I thought was the love of my life. I remember *crying* and *singing* this song at the top of my lungs. I even remember the smell of that old car, the color of the sky, and the feeling of the wind rushing through the open windows, blowing the tears and snot off my face as I sobbed my eyes out. Do you get a sense of what I experienced just by reading my description?

At that time, in my 17-year-old life, I was devastated. And not only was I devastated because my boyfriend left me, the more critical aspect was the meaning – the *interpretation* - I applied to my boyfriend's leaving me. The bloodhounds had started with, and strengthened, this wiring over the years with Little-Kimmy that I wasn't *special* enough. Can you see how I would continue with this interpretation that I wasn't *special* or acceptable enough? To think differently wouldn't naturally be available to me, even as an adult, without awareness. The song was all it took for me to feel that moment again.

By the time we become aware of this process, the mental and emotional wiring are already strongly embedded. It will take an intentional act of rewiring. Hopefully this is what you are desiring and why you are willing to look "under your bed" at this point.

Rewiring Strategies

The rewiring strategies will vary based on the depth and strength of the current wiring. As I addressed with the monster tracks, sometimes it just takes a quick mental shift to release the power of a specific track and we can move on. Other things may require stronger ammunition.

Sometime in my 40's, I developed a fear of flying. I don't remember having a traumatic experience. All I know is that I became afraid – petrified. So, in response, I started **educating** myself about flight and commercial flying. I read statistics about how safe flying was. I looked and thought about the thousands of planes all over the world every day that don't crash.

I Googled the last time a commercial plane had crashed. I talked to pilots, who told me about the laws of aerodynamics regarding lift, thrust, gravity, and drag. They told me how safe the commercial airplanes of today are. They told me about the many safety measures in place before a customer even gets on the plane. The odds of crashing in a commercial plane were miniscule, I learned.

Slowly, the knowledge I gained led me to *run to the roar* and get back on a plane again. I felt the monster, Amy triggered, and chatter screaming. I took deep breaths to settle Amy down, and I used the information my logical brain had learned to communicate with it.

I reassured Amy that we were better off in a commercial plane than in a car; that hundreds of thousands of people fly every day on commercial airplanes, and they **don't** crash; that the safety checks were extensive and not at the hand of just one worker on the ground; that pilots have thousands of hours of experience, and they love to fly. If it were dangerous, they and the flight attendants wouldn't be doing this for a living.

And now, I love flying. Flying is one of my most favorite things to do. I even have fun in turbulence because I told myself a new story about all the bumps I was experiencing. (Think: paper airplane!)

Physically, there is no difference between the feeling of *excitement* getting on a *fun* roller coaster and the *fear* I had getting on an airplane. Our heart beats faster. We get a little sweaty and feel butterflies in our stomach. Fear and excitement share the same physical symptoms, so what's the difference? Whatever it is that we tell ourselves about it. The difference is how we approach it. Because my desire to travel was stronger than my fear of flying, I, consciously, rewired my brain.

Is knowledge enough? Knowledge alone doesn't do diddly-squat. Sure, it can open the door, but it's when you *use* the knowledge, with some of the tools I'm referring to, that you can accomplish the rewiring process.

The I AM Strategy

This is the most exciting part of the book for me. This tool is necessary to deal with the **deeper wiring** that takes stronger ammunition, so to speak. This continues to be my main strategy for rewiring. It was born in the depths of my soul. It lives in my *knowing* place; the knowing that is as real as breathing.

I AM represents three things:

1) **Identify**

2) **Awareness**

3) **Meditation**

Identify

Up to this point in the book, we have explored *identifying* our potential monster tracks. We can now use our prefrontal cortex brain to reason and apply logic to our deep beliefs and struggles. *Identifying is the first step.* We can decide which thoughts receive our focus and emotion and we can choose to tell a new story and create a new interpretation of life.

Awareness

I have mentioned several times throughout this book that the purpose of this work is to grow in our awareness. I had someone tell me during their *monster hunting* process, "Kim – sheesh! Enough already. I can only handle so much awareness!"

Yes, awareness can be bittersweet. In fact, like cleaning out a closet, it gets messier before it gets better. Be prepared for that. Once you are willing to look, you will see many things that will make you uncomfortable. There have been times in my life where I want to *throw up* because of what I become aware of inside myself.

If you want to test your awareness ability, just set an intention to grow, to become **more**. As soon as that reality hits your brain, obstacles will **immediately** show up; you will notice firsthand which of the monster tracks are running in the background. In fact, I think of life as our training ground, where we get **firsthand** lessons and practice for developing ourselves. Our families and close relationships provide us with an intense boot camp for our personal development. My friend, Janet, called this our *"heavenly sandpaper!"*

With regard to family, here's an example of a common spousal conflict, highlighting the power (and pain) of awareness:

Your Spouse:

"Can't you ever be on time to anything?"

You:

"I would have been ready if I hadn't had to go back and lock up the house."

(Awareness Alert! Button track! Blame track! Maybe Perfection track if the house isn't locked up "just so"...)

Your Spouse:
"You were late even before that.
You are ALWAYS late!"

You:
"We DON'T need to be there 10 minutes early – so I am not late! It's ALWAYS this way. Your entire family is OCD about arriving to things early. Then you blame me for being late!"

(Awareness Alert! Increased button track! Judgment track! all or nothing track!)

If you are able to catch yourself and then shift in the **middle** of the conflict, good for you. If you can't, be gentle with yourself. Awareness is tricky because it can trigger the judgment track.

The person who said to me "Enough with awareness already" was having a hard time **not** beating themselves up when they noticed themselves slipping into old routines. The difference now is that they **know** they are doing it. They **know** their button is pushed. They **know** they are blaming. They **know** they are judging. Prior to their awareness, they ran on autopilot. It was just **that's the way I am**. It was understandable - because of *others'* behavior.

You can "aware" yourself to death! Hopefully, this is temporary. The point is to move to be an observer of your monster tracks and not **justify OR judge** them.

When a monster track shows up, we can shift to gratitude instead. We can think - *Interesting how I got my button pushed and jumped immediately to blame and judgment.*

I will be ready next time with a more empowering response. Thank you, (spouse, universe, life), for showing me this area to work on.

Meditation

This is the **granddaddy** of rewiring tools. Einstein discovered that "We can't solve problems by using the same kind of thinking we used when we created them." This ends up being the conundrum we face when we start the process of rewiring. Our thoughts will lead us back into the deep grooves of our familiar thoughts and feelings.

The doorway to meditation is breathing. From a physiological standpoint, deep belly breathing impacts your parasympathetic nervous system. Physically, you'll feel calmer as you start breathing from your belly. It's interesting that the word "inspire" literally means to *breathe in*. When you breathe, try and breathe from the deepest place in your body. To find your *belly breath*, lie flat on the floor, on your back, straight legged. You will automatically find the deep breath from this place. Your tummy will extend; but don't judge – it's perfect!

The only thing necessary here is that while you breathe, notice your thoughts **without judging** them, and then bring your attention back to your breath. When I unwired my fear of flying, I needed to breathe deeply. As long as I breathed deeply and quoted the knowledge of what I had learned to Amy, I was calm.

Without the deep breathing, I would have been fighting an uphill battle.

Breathing has **actual** biological, psychological, and physiological power. It is a little-known tool in our natural tool chest. Early on in my meditation practice, I told myself messages that *Little Kimmy* needed to hear. On the inhale I would say in my mind, "*I am.*" I would hold it for a mindful pause, then exhale slowly, and then say whatever *new truth* came to mind. For me, initially, it was the word "loved." Find whatever word produces a **strong** emotional response. This is key!

That word will speak directly to your still scared young self: *I am...worthy. I am...acceptable.* At first it could be extremely emotional. It needs to be emotional to re-wire. Remember? What fires together - that means what creates emotions, starts connecting the brain waves. If you do this activity often, you will "wire" what you have "fired."

Observe, breathe, and love yourself.

Pay no attention to chatter, if you hear it. It is normal. Don't believe or argue with it. Observe, breathe, and love yourself. Over time, you will accept the love, and will start feeling it, deep inside you. This is a self-directed process for each person.

A typical exercise at my events is to help attendees learn this tool. We actually lower the lights, focus on our breathing, and then we visualize and affirm the truth to which we are rewiring. The reports of those who felt **instant** emotional relief and those who continued in this practice and watched themselves transform, were overwhelming. Dr. Joe Dispenza wrote a book titled *Breaking the Habit of Being Yourself*. He does a deep dive showing the actual brain-wave patterns as we meditate, setting a clear intention while going to a positive emotion. It is fantastic to see on an fMRI scan the proof of what is happening inside our brains. It shows how the rewiring *tangibly* occurs. We can literally decide who we want to be and recreate ourselves.

Visualization

I have also seen what happens when we use our *mind's eye* to *emotionally* create a new reality of ourselves. We can infuse ourselves with compassion. We can then be in the perfect environment, brain-wise, to *feel* ourselves into a new reality.

Bring up vividly imagined pictures in your mind of how you would like to feel in any given situation. See, and more importantly, **FEEL** yourself experiencing it *right now*. As I have laid out, your unconscious mind cannot tell the difference between a vividly imagined thought and what is true in your reality. Again, if the thought is real enough to produce an emotion, either negative or positive, it's real enough to fire brain waves.

You want to be happy? Practice seeing, feeling, hearing, *happy* in your meditation. Create images and situations *in your imagination* that make you FEEL happy.

Smile, on purpose. Even if you don't feel like it, smiling can shift your energy and bring the *happy* feeling.

You want to be well? See, hear, and feel the *feeling of* how you would feel IF you were well. Would you be grateful? Can you find something about your body right now to be grateful for? Find the *feeling* of gratitude - even if it's for having a pinky toe. It can start a cascade of gratitude. Milk that feeling as long as you can.

Do you want to be loved? Find pictures in your mind's eye of you being unconditionally loved by someone (Your spouse, your parent, God, The Universe, your Dog). I have also found that *feeling* love for the "little-you" can help you find the love for the *current* you. Go for the *feeling* of how you want your entire life to be, but don't wait to see it externally. Create that *feeling.* Pretend you have it, if necessary, to begin with. That can work!

When I first started practicing meditation, I had a singular event that changed my life in every way. I refer to it as my *Love Epiphany.*

This epiphany came during a dark chapter in our family. We were going through a hard time with one of our children. One day, as I was practicing the breathing technique that I described above – while I was saying my affirmation, *I am...loved* – an **image** came to my mind of my dad holding *me* in a rocking chair. He was stroking my hair and asking how my day was. He was telling me over and over how much he loved me. I felt a complete love infusion of every cell. It just washed over me. I can't even describe it; there are no words.

This feeling created a healing in my brain, an instant rewiring, it seemed. Remember, it was my relationship with my dad that played a large role in my monster creation. The mental image of him loving me evoked a deep emotional response. Fear lived in my imagination as a child, so it was in my imagination where the healing needed to occur.

My wounded wiring was then rewired. I instantly felt unconditionally loved, and my life was changed in the "twinkling of an eye." Since then, my meditation practice has continually evolved. What I have noticed over the years are my *go-to* thoughts are fundamentally different. I find myself more loving, kind, aware, and nonreactive.

Please don't confuse this as being perfect. As I've alluded to earlier, we are continually "unpeeling" our damaged "onion." A couple of years into this practice, for example, I was in a situation with someone in business who continued to push my buttons. She was the type of person who just rubbed me the wrong way; every time she opened her mouth, I wanted to hurt her. She wielded a good amount of influence, which also pushed my button.

I found myself going back and forth between *flight* (*Dang it – she IS better than I am!*) and *fight* (*I've got to prove her wrong!*), and I also found myself continually arguing with her in my mind. I was even talking about her behind her back. One day, during my meditation, the thought came to me – **Am I willing to see her differently?** This thought stung, but then it stuck. I decided to change my interpretation.

"How can I see her differently?"

Once I **sincerely** opened up to that possibility, ideas and thoughts came flooding in. I saw her heart. I saw how, in her way, she meant well. She had the best intentions. It was an immediate shift of energy for me. From that day on, I never felt any more animosity toward her. I couldn't. I remembered how I felt and how much angst I had in the past, but it seemed like a distant memory. My negative feelings were gone. I believe this ability was directly tied to my newly rewired brain.

There are so many self-guided meditations to choose from. I've had many people say to me, "Kim, I just can't seem to meditate. I don't think it's for me. I can't quiet my mind." I chuckle inside because I hear the chatter loud and clear.

Do you think anyone can do it naturally or easily?

Nope. If they could, they wouldn't be reading this or any other self-help book. They would naturally be rewired and have peace.

Happy Hunting!

My goals with this book were to help you determine: if you had a monster under your "bed;" to show how it was created; to expose the purpose of this monster; and to show what to do about it. If this metaphor makes sense to you, I hope it gives you a sense of peace. I hope you've uncovered some scary things inside you. I hope you *love* them, because you now understand they are *you*.

I hope you realize the voice telling you that you are not *enough* is the voice of your childhood self. I hope you can see where that deep feeling of dread running in your psyche's operating system, comes from. I hope you realize you are not a flawed creation. I hope you have the courage to take action and do the **heavy lifting** of rewiring your brain.

My hopes are not just for you, but for your **family**, your **children**, your **community**, and your **world.** The ripples that expand from *you* leave their energy on everything you touch. You are an individual of intrinsic, valuable worth to all the people in your life. You are a **miracle**. *You are needed.*

As you go through this rewiring process, the more you accept love for yourself and *feel* it – not just *know* it logically – your child self will heal as it knows and *accepts* unconditional love. This will shift your energy source to the wind and sail. And you can begin living in more freedom with a sense of who you **truly** are. Everything and everyone in your life will be impacted. The peace and love you've been searching for is waiting for you right beside *the monster under your bed.*

About The Author

Kim Fiske is a respected speaker, life coach, author and thought-leader who is sought after for her ability to convey to audiences provocative concepts and practical ways to deal with what she has coined as the "monster under the bed".

She has been able to change the way people view their relationships, career, life goals & journey by giving them the ability to acknowledge their proverbial "monster" while providing mechanisms for coping with it.

Her blend of pure authenticity, professional but approachable accessibility, and intuitive and down-to-earth nature makes her desirable as a life coach for individuals looking for answers to how to take their personal growth and self-awareness beyond where it has currently evolved to a greater place of self-actualization and reflection. Kim's enthusiasm, humor, insights and passion for life combined with her practical experience and applications can help show individuals how to make life the best it can be and one that is further enriched.

Kim has earned over 25 years of experience training and coordinating a team of entrepreneurial leaders in industries such as health and wellness, mentorship and personal coaching with an emphasis on business strategy and development.

She is a Neuro-Linguistic Programming (NLP) Practitioner, Certified Coach of Life Planning (CCLP), a 7-figure Income Earner in Relationship Marketing, Member of The Association of Network Marketing Professionals, Member of the National Speakers Association, eWomen Network Platinum Member, PRO Member of The Association of Network Marketing Professionals and a Member of the American Business Women's Association

Kim spends time with her husband Joe at their homes in Nevada and Oregon. They have four children and five grandchildren.

For more information about Kim and how she can help you, visit **www.kimfiske.com**

Made in the USA
Coppell, TX
09 October 2020